CATHOUSE

OR

THE HOUSE OF ALL NATIONS

A Comedy of Eros

By

Hiag Akmakjian

March 5, 2017

ISBN 978-0-9847249-5-6

ACT I

It is the start of the work day at The House of All Nations. It is a brothel-ranch in Acacia, Nevada, just outside Las Vegas. We see two rooms. One is a small parlor that serves as a business office and discreet supply room for condoms, fresh linens and whatever other materials are needed in the operation of a high-class brothel. A bank of video screens are connected to hidden cameras in each of the girls' "party rooms".

Side by side with the parlor is the other room, an old-fashioned bar where clientele are received and can have a drink if they wish before choosing a girl and going into one of the rooms. Behind the bar, there is a very large Toulouse-Lautrec reproduction of a Parisian brothel scene. Between the two rooms, a passageway leads somewhere to the rear where the women entertain their clients.

Zoe, the Madam, is conducting her daily staff conference in the business office. It is early afternoon of Christmas eve and the office-study looks festive with a small Christmas tree, holly wreaths and holiday decorations.

Mme. Zoe is comfortably seated in her Eames chair and has gathered her staff around her. She is serving tea as she discusses the agenda for the afternoon and evening with the girls, DESIREE, CORAL and DAWN, who are scantily clad – respectable but ready for work. NICOLE is a bartender and acts as Mme. Zoe's assistant. She is not one of the girls. She's at the bar and does not attend these meetings.

Another member of the staff, HYACINTH, is temporarily absent, being with a client in one of the rooms.

The tea is served by Dawn on an ornate family heirloom silver platter on which are incongruously placed some cardboard picnic plates with cheap little Oreo cookies. A second tray bears long pastry-like cheese sticks suggestive of penises. With zest, Zoe bites off a piece of cheese stick and begins her power-breakfast pep talk.

ZOE

Close the door. No, leave it open. It gets stuffy in here.

From across the hall, in the lounge, NICOLE, minding the shop, as it were, answers a ringing phone and yells over to Zoe.

NICOLE

It's Avery. Wants to speak to you.

ZOE

(quietly to DAWN, seated beside her) Please pass the cream.

NICOLE

(yells over again) Zoe?

ZOE

Sugar.

NICOLE

Zoe, it's Avery.

ZOE

(yells to NICOLE) Kindly inform the prick I'll return his call later.

NICOLE

He says he heard that.

ZOE

One more lump, please.

NICOLE

And he wants to know when.

ZOE

Kindly inform him probably never.

NICOLE

He says it's a very pressing matter.

ZOE

Kindly tell him to go press himself.

NICOLE

(*says something into the phone and hangs up*)

ZOE

(*Turning back to the others and continuing with what she had been saying.*) Before we start this afternoon, two announcements. One is that Jack Tully will be here this afternoon and wants to make it a big one this time – as many of you young ladies as are available, plus he'll bring two of his favorite Las Vegas escorts with him. As a reminder: the last time he was here he spent $75,000. Ordinarily, this being Christmas eve, today would be a slow day, so there shouldn't be a problem catering to him, so let's make him feel welcome. And besides, quite frankly, we could use the business. Next: we've booked Mr. Anderson.

DAWN

The crossdresser?

ZOE

He prefers transvestite. And there's our dear Mr. Lowell Goodson, he's booked for a threesome, so Coral and Desiree?

CORAL

He had she and I the last time.

ZOE

(*under her breath*) He had me and her. (*Then in a normal voice*) Whatever you did, he liked it, because he specifically asked for you. And then there's Randy McPhee –

DESIREE

Who's he?

ZOE

He's the one who wants his girl to nurse on a baby bottle and ignore him while he's doing her – and make sure the nipple on the bottle is fresh this time. He said it looked disgusting the last time, two inches from his nose. And then there's Fat Harold, the piss freak.

DAWN

Ewww.

ZOE

He'll choose from the lineup. He says he doesn't like to piss on the same girl twice. He says it's too cruel. So please, ladies, let's not comment – we're here to provide a service, not pass judgment. OK? Everybody got all that?

DAWN

No rim jobs, I hope.

ZOE

Not today. And the other announcement is this: you'll be hearing rumors that we're being shut down by those creeps – what are they called again? The Family Above All.

DAWN

The *what*?

ZOE

Family Above All. Just some well-intentioned nuts, otherwise known as do-gooders. And I want everybody to know we're not.

DESIREE

We're not what?

ZOE

Not closing. We're still open and will foreseeably remain open. We're here to serve the community, so quash that rumor if it comes up. As a full-service provider it is our firm belief that sex will always have its way, whether it's Christmas or Mother's Day or the end of the world, and we're number one in that field. . . . Oh and remember, politeness and courtesy are our specialty. We're the best in the county and, uh, Dawn? Would you please knock it off about having once made it with George Clooney's cousin Albert. You know it's not true. He doesn't *have* a cousin Albert. I googled it. Any questions?

DAWN

If it's such a marvelous service we're performing for our oh so wonderful community, how come our oh so wonderful community considers it a criminal offense?

CORAL

It's the puritans among us – you know, the ones with the dirty minds.

ZOE

There's nothing new about good women doing prostitution. Farmer's wives have always helped out when times were bad. I had a friend once who sent her daughter to Radcliffe that way.

CORAL

I like performing a good service for society. As long as society wears a condom. Who's this Jack Dolly who's been asking for me?

ZOE

Jack Tully. Yes, you're new here and he likes 'em new. Nicole will fill you in.

CORAL

Is he into kink?

DESIREE

Yeah, he's fun. He sometimes likes dressing up as one of the girls. He did that once and pretended he works here. But it was all just for laughs. He's all man.

CORAL

Hey! He likes dressing? Cool! That's not kink, that's good taste. I've got a touch of lesbo, so I'll take him.

ZOE

He likes to be corrupted, he says. That's just a joke.

CORAL

Corruption was my major in college. You should have seen our dorm!

ZOE

Then you should go into politics. There's nothing corrupting in sex. Sex doesn't corrupt anybody – not among adults. Only money corrupts.

As the women get up and walk out . . .

DAWN

I could do with a little more corruption.

CORAL

At Radcliffe we had the hottest sorority in New England. Sigma Pi. We used to call it Eat My Pie.

Girls drift out toward the lounge bar and take up their positions, slightly bored with the inevitable waiting around for the first clients to show up. As they leave, DAWN is heard to say meditatively:

DAWN

Hmmm. Radcliffe.

Already seated at the bar is Dikran, swarthy, neatly dressed, trying to be discreet, as though he's not really there. Seated on the stool at the end of the bar is Phil, the bouncer. Behind the bar, Nicole, who manages the place for Zoe, is busy with the usual preopening bar preparations.

NICOLE

(*to PHIL*): You look bright and cheerful. Looking for something special?

PHIL

Yes, the bluebird of happiness.

NICOLE

Fresh out of bluebirds. How about a little eggnog for my favorite bouncer? (*Ladles a cup from a large cut-crystal bowl*) Early to be on duty, isn't it, with nobody around?

PHIL

Crap day.

NICOLE

Anything new in Vegas?

PHIL

Crap Vegas.

NICOLE

Yeah.

PHIL

Empedocles.

NICOLE

Emp - who?

PHIL

- pedocles. A great, supergreat philosopher.

NICOLE

Never heard of him.

PHIL

He said that everything was earth, fire, air and water.

NICOLE

Uh-hunh.

PHIL

And that what held it all together was love.

NICOLE

Nuts. (*Holds out a small plate.*)

PHIL

Democritus said the goal of life is cheerfulness. Of course the two don't necessarily contradict each other. Salted?

NICOLE

That's what Zoe's Old-Fashioned Cathouse is all about. Make people cheerful. Without salt.

PHIL

Depends on how you define "cheerfulness".

NICOLE

Yeah, there's always that to mull over, isn't there?

PHIL

Depends on how you define "mull over".

CORAL

(*chiming in*) We're all a happy family here.

NICOLE

Yeah. All happy families are alike.

PHIL

So is shit, pretty much.

CORAL

What's wrong with him?

NICOLE

He's on one of his philosophical kicks – you know how he gets. Traumatic weaning, pulled away from mother's tit too soon. . . .

CORAL

Yeah? I'd be happy to let him compensate for it. My tits have been aching lately.

> *A male scream is heard from one of the bedrooms. It could be an orgasm or a death throe.*

NICOLE

You want a kid?

CORAL

Bring a kid into this crappy world?

> *The male scream is heard again. The two women pause in their talk, listening. They know what it is.*

CORAL

(*quietly*) Must be Harvey. Hyacinth really knows how to make a guy happy.

> *Another silence.*

I guess that's about it for old Harve.

NICOLE

No, he's good for two. We really should get that room sound-proofed. Have you ever had Harve?

CORAL

Can't say I've had the pleasure.

NICOLE

The girls say he has a schwanz and a half.

CORAL

(*dreamily*) Hmmm.

NICOLE

Sometimes too big is no good, y'know?

CORAL

Speak for yourself. Have you ever had one that was too big?

NICOLE

Yeah. My father's.

CORAL

You were abused? How *AW*-ful!

NICOLE

Not really. Except in the sense that it makes everybody else's schwanz fall short of the mark.

CORAL

(*thrilled at the thought*) Wow!

DESIREE

Moves over and sits next to Dikran.

Hi. Mind if I join you? My name's Desiree.

DIKRAN

No.

DESIREE

You look intellectual.

DIKRAN

Who, me?

DESIREE

You look like somebody from the East.

DIKRAN

East Fresno.

DESIREE

I could tell right away. You get starved for somebody to talk to. Do you like me?

DIKRAN

On a sample of fifteen seconds, I can honestly say, uh – I like your smile.

DESIREE

That's sweet. How would you like to buy a girl a drink?

DIKRAN

Sure. What'll you have?

DESIREE

Double martini rocks. You?

DIKRAN

I'll have, let's see, a ginger ale on the rocks.

NICOLE

(*wryly*) Don't tell me – you're drivin', right?

Makes the drinks.

DESIREE

Tanqueray, with a twist. It's my favorite drink. You get a nice high and you get it fast.

DIKRAN

You like things fast.

DESIREE

Fast and loose. Just thinking of a martini gets me high.

PHIL

That should not only spare eventual damage to your liver but meanwhile promote great clarity of thought – should a thought ever occur.

DIKRAN

Should what?

DESIREE

Don't mind Phil. He's a little crazy in the head.

DIKRAN

Listen, Philip.

DESIREE

His name's not Philip. We call him Phil, short for philosopher. And don't mind him.

PHIL

Yeah, don't mind me.

DESIREE

He's just a little crazy but in a nice way. Desert fever or something. I don't think all his switches are working.

PHIL

In the old days, people used to talk about you behind your back.

DESIREE

He thinks that everything that has ever happened has already happened someplace else. We're just reenacting it here.

PHIL

Sort of Platonic in a weird way.

DESIREE

Sounds crazy to me.

PHIL

Hey listen, Plato was no asshole.

DESIREE

He was an ancient Greek, wasn't he?

PHIL

He believed in the transforming power of love.

DESIREE

That's not my thing per say.

> *Nicole places the drinks in front of DIKRAN and*
> *DESIREE. Hers is plain water disguised as a*
> *drink.*

DESIREE

(*to Dikran*) You sound like the kind of person I could enjoy talking with. Where you from?

DIKRAN

You already asked me that. I'm still from Fresno. East Fresno.

DESIREE
Think you'd like to get to know me better?

DIKRAN
Yes I would. I'd like to know the story I heard about being shut down. Is this place closing?

DESIREE
No, that's just talk. It's those people again.

DIKRAN
It's what people again?

DESIREE
The Family Above All people. Pain in the butt above all, if you ask me. Hypocrites.

DIKRAN
Why do they want to close it down?

DESIREE
Every time there's a mayor's election they have a clean-up drive.

DIKRAN
The mayor wants to close this place?

NICOLE
Oh no, Stan's OK. He's one of our best clients.

DIKRAN
Stanley Brinkerhoff the mayor comes here?

NICOLE
He's a regular.

DIKRAN
Have you had him?

NICOLE
Me? No. I just work the bar. But the girls all have.

DIKRAN
What's he like?

DESIREE
If Stanley does with his wife what he does with me, she deserves a crwah de guerre.

DIKRAN

In and out?

DESIREE

Behind his back they call him Slam-Bam-Stan.

DIKRAN

And thank-you-mam?

DESIREE

Not even. That would amount to a romance, coming from him.

DIKRAN

What about the sheriff?

NICOLE

Dennis? He's a man and a half. He not only has a schwanz, he knows what to do with it to please the ladies.

DESIREE

Yeah, and no brain. Me, I'd prefer a man with a brain and no schwanz.

NICOLE

What the hell good is a man without a schwanz? And without schwanzes, where would we all be?

DESIREE

I meant if I was to get married.

DIKRAN

You would marry a man with no schwanz?

DESIREE

There are other ways.

NICOLE

Dildos. A dildo is a schwanz without a man.

DESIREE

A dildo is a man without back talk. Or dirty socks.

NICOLE

Oh yeah? When did a dildo ever take you out to dinner?

DESIREE

You've got a point there. But I'm sure Apple will come up with something.

PHIL

Ladies, ladies.

DIKRAN

You planning on getting married?

DESIREE

Someday, maybe. Find the right guy.

DIKRAN

That's very commendable.

DESIREE

Well, you know, I'd have to look out for myself if we ever closed down.

NICOLE

We're not closing down. Cathouses never fold. They temporarily close until the heat's off.

DIKRAN

Didn't you say the mayor's one of your better clients?

NICOLE

He's not the one who's causing the trouble. It's the Family Above All creeps. And I've heard rumors about some trouble Crawford has gotten Zoe into.

DIKRAN

Who's Crawford?

NICOLE

The big cheese.

DESIREE

Numero uno.

NICOLE

He's a very wealthy man. A banker. He used to be a big customer a few years ago. Zoe won't let him near the place now.

DIKRAN

How come?

NICOLE

Lover's spat.

DIKRAN

A lover's spat? Here?

NICOLE

He insulted her. He told her she was so fat that when she pulled her drawers down, her ass was still in them.

DESIREE

He never said that! Fat?! She's perfectly normal. I mean for someone her age. That's cruel. It's just simply not true.

NICOLE

That's hate for you. It distorts perception.

PHIL

Perception is a slippery concept in philosophy. Of course, it all depends on how you define "perception".

DIKRAN

You know, usually when there's a lot of rumors going around about a place closing down there's some truth in it.

DESIREE

They're not closing this place down.

DIKRAN

Well, you know, the will of the people . . .

DESIREE

What people? Half the town is our clientele. Some people'd be homeless without us.

NICOLE

The only way you could close a cathouse down is by opening up another one, so you might as well keep the first one going.

DESIREE

Tell that to Crawford. He says the way to keep this place open is to get the goods on one of the old biddies of Family Above All.

DIKRAN

You mean, catch them with *their* pants down?

NICOLE

Their pants don't come down.

DESIREE

Everybody's pants come down.

NICOLE

Maybe we could put the screws on Brinkerhoff?

DIKRAN

Put the screws on the mayor?

NICOLE

Stan's our greatest client. Stanley Brinkerhoff, mayor of our fair city.

DESIREE

Town.

CORAL

Hamlet.

NICOLE

Ranch. Anyway, he's the one stirring up the trouble about vice.

DESIREE

He sure doesn't talk like that when his mouth is full of peroxide blond.

NICOLE

(*laughs*) You are what you eat.

DESIREE

He's very oral. He's going around telling everybody that there's moral decay eating away at the very fiber of our being.

NICOLE

I'm surprised all his teeth haven't decayed.

DESIREE

He's particularly partial to Coral's furry little checkbook, which is his cornball way of referring to pussy.

NICOLE

She's shaved now.

DESIREE

Is nothing sacred?

DIKRAN

(*goes and sits next to PHIL at the bar*) A place like this can give you a whole new slant on civilization.

PHIL

Depends on how you define "slant" and how you define "civilization".

Enter MALCOLM. He's a handsome young man. He's wearing a white hospital uniform and, oddly juxtaposed, a sporty-looking cowboy hat and is carrying an important-looking attaché case.

MALCOLM

Excuse me.

NICOLE

Hi, cowboy. Hey, your first time here?

MALCOLM

Uh, I'm not exactly a cowboy. Uh, I'm here with the report for Ms. Muhlbach.

NICOLE

You mean Mme. Zoe. Who are you?

MALCOLM

I'm a nurse-examiner. You know, for the county.

NICOLE

Which county?

MALCOLM

Clark County. I'm in the Public Health, Safety, Prevention and Medical Research Center of Greater Las Vegas.

NICOLE

Sounds like a fancy name for a clap clinic. I'll take it.

MALCOLM

It isn't a clap clinic. It's the Public Health, Safety, Prevention and Medical Research Center of Greater Las Vegas. I'm supposed to give it to Madame Zoe in person. It's confidential.

NICOLE

Here, I'll take care of this. Zoe told me to bring it to her when it arrives. If there's any clap going around she wants to know about it fast.

MALCOLM

You sure? Because I wouldn't want to get anybody in trouble. You know, have it get into the wrong hands.

NICOLE

These are the results of the piss samples, right?

MALCOLM

Uh, I'm not allowed to say. But I wouldn't look at the written report if I were you.

NICOLE

Why not?

MALCOLM

It's – uh – well, I'm not supposed to say.

NICOLE

You mean it's not good?

MALCOLM

I'm not allowed to say.

NICOLE

You're joking!

MALCOLM

I'm deeply sorry, Miss.

NICOLE

You're joking!

MALCOLM

I know it's not about you personally.

NICOLE

Who's it about?

MALCOLM

Looks at paper.

Two, uh, women.

NICOLE

Here, let me have that.

MALCOLM

OK. Just don't look at the names.

NICOLE

Promise.

She starts to leave with the paper, obviously reading the names as she goes and saying as she exits:

Holy shit!

More screams – from Harvey. Malcolm looks around him, nervous and unhappy and a little anxious.

DESIREE

Hey, cowboy.

MALCOLM

I'm not really a cowboy. I just bought this cowboy hat to –

DESIREE

You out here from Vegas?

MALCOLM

Yes, ma'am.

DESIREE

Bet you see a lot of interesting things in your line of work.

MALCOLM

Not really.

DESIREE

Why don't you take off that uniform and make yourself comfortable?

MALCOLM

I'm only wearing underwear underneath. And I don't like to show people my underwear. Besides I have to be getting back.

DESIREE

Oh, too bad. You're kinda cute.

MALCOLM

Thank you. So if that'll be all, I'll be leaving now.

DESIREE

Be seeing you.

MALCOLM

Goodbye, ma'am.

As Malcolm leaves, Harvey emerges from one of the rooms in the back, hair disheveled. He is a mulatto and at the moment is looking very happy.

HARVEY

Tasty little morsel.

DESIREE

Yeah, that Hyacinth's something.

HARVEY

Might be in the mood for seconds tonight.

DESIREE

It sounded like you were having seconds in there now.

HARVEY

(remembering) Yeah, wow. OK, maybe thirds.

DESIREE

(*looks at HARVEY and DIKRAN*) That's what this fine establishment is all about.

Hyacinth appears and slips quietly onto a seat at the bar.

DESIREE

(*to Harvey*) Hi, I'm Desiree.

HARVEY

Hello, Desiree.

DESIREE

So you're having a good time.

3/5/2017

21

HARVEY

I sure am. But my friend here, Dikran, is not.

DESIREE

He's OK. We were just having a drink together.

HARVEY

He doesn't want to get laid.

DESIREE

Really? Don't you like anybody here?

HARVEY

(*looking at the women, who all smile seductively at him*) Oh it's not that. He's in mourning. His wife left him.

DESIREE

Oh, that's so sad. This place'll cheer him up, though.

HARVEY

I doubt it.

DESIREE

It's our specialty. The House of Happy Endings.

HARVEY

He utterly refuses to be cheered up.

DESIREE

Well, it's a pretty hard blow after all, you know, a wife walking out on you. But then, you never know, she might come back.

DIKRAN

She's *never* coming back.

HARVEY

She ran off with a lion tamer.

DESIREE

A *lion* tamer! Wow!

HARVEY

In the circus. If you ask me, she's got a little S and M in her blood. (*To DIKRAN*) Why don't you be a sport and give Desiree here a little, you know, have a – you know –

DIKRAN

No, look, I came here because you wanted company. Don't start pestering me.

HARVEY

But it's not natural to not want to get laid.

DESIREE

(to HARVEY) Who would you recommend for your friend?

HARVEY

Hyacinth. Or – hey, I know – Coral. She's really hot in the sack.

DESIREE

Yeah, she comes recommended.

HARVEY

She really comes too.

DESIREE

Would you like Coral?

DIKRAN

No, thank you.

DESIREE

You look so sad.

HARVEY

All Armenians look sad. They all got wiped out.

DESIREE

You an Armenian? I never had an Armenian. I thought you said you were from Fresno.

HARVEY

You're wasting your time. He's down in the dumps and he's angry. Anybody who comes to a cathouse and doesn't want to get laid is no longer a rational human being. Especially an Armenian.

DIKRAN

People aren't always rational, you know.

PHIL

Depends how you define "rational".

HARVEY

Yeah, tell me about it.

DIKRAN

(*wearily*) I just came to keep you company, remember?

HARVEY

I thought you'd change your mind once you were here and saw all these fine young ladies.

DESIREE

Don't be so hard on the poor guy.

HARVEY

A hard-on this poor guy doesn't have. He's suffering for the millions of his countrymen who were killed.

DESIREE

They were killed? I didn't see anything on the news.

HARVEY

Nineteen-fifteen.

DESIREE

Nineteen-fif-*teen?* I thought you were talking about the evening news.

> *An outside door is heard closing. YITZAKH walks in, nods to the others, sits at the bar.*

HARVEY

They didn't have the evening news in those days.

DESIREE

Hi (*to the newcomer YITZAKH*).

YITZAKH

Hi.

HARVEY

The Turks killed a million and a half of them.

YITZAKH

Killed who?

HARVEY

Armenians.

YITZAKH

Death. Everywhere death. Millions of my countrymen were killed too.

HARVEY

What country you from?

YITZAKH

I'm from the U.S. of A. But I'm talking about Auschwitz – the Jews.

DESIREE

Oh, you a Jewish fellow?

YITZAKH

Yes.

DESIREE

Oh, Happy Hanukkah.

YITZAKH

Thank you. And a Happy Christmas to you.

HARVEY

I'm very sorry about your people.

DESIREE

Yes. Who knows how many Einsteins there would have been among them.

YITZAKH

Never mind Einstein. There were six million people among them. Every human being is an Einstein.

HARVEY

But you, at least, you're able to put it behind you. Life goes on.

YITZAKH

I'm not too sure about that. Do you read the papers?

HARVEY

The Middle East.

YITZAKH

A hot bed – all violence and hate.

HARVEY

Yes but my people, we're still suffering.

DIKRAN

What do you mean you're still suffering? You're not black. You look like a mulatto, you're only half black. What people? You're a dentist. You make a fat living. And look at you, *you're* fat too. The only suffering you're going through is dealing with your obesity.

HARVEY

Racism is what I'm suffering from.

DIKRAN

But you're lucky. If Americans hadn't of brought you people over from Africa and given you jobs and food and shelter on plantations, you'd be living in grass huts now. And where would the invention of the blues be? You'd still be beating tom toms and contracting AIDS all over the place.

HARVEY

What are you talking about? You some kind of racist?

DIKRAN

They didn't have saxophones and pianos in jungles. You got all that *here*. That's what I'm talking about. Without our musical instruments you'd be nowhere.

HARVEY

Are you for real?

DIKRAN

Yeah I'm for real. Don't bullshit me. You got a rich heritage over here. You have slavery to brag about and get sympathy from whites. It's the best thing that ever happened to you.

HARVEY

(*happily*) He's getting mad! He's coming back to life!

DIKRAN

My people were *wiped out*. They're all dead. Whereas you, in a hundred and fifty years you went from cotton-picking slaves to tennis and golf champs.

HARVEY

You know what you are? You're full of shit.

DIKRAN

From slavery to Mercedes. We made you into millionaires and football players. And our people are dead.

HARVEY

So what are you, a ghost?

DIKRAN

And now you want to sue insurance companies for trillions of dollars. The whites gave you a high standard of living and you want to sue them for reparations.

HARVEY

I can't believe I'm hearing this shit.

DIKRAN

Blacks secretly take pride in their slavery. It gives them status. White people feel guilt, which is an added pleasure. In your heart of hearts you're glad to have your history to brag about. You didn't suffer. The people *before* you suffered but you get all the glory.

DESIREE

Hey you guys, take it easy.

HARVEY

You should be glad the Turks killed the Armenians. If it hadn't been for that, you'd still be in the back hills of Anatolia.

DIKRAN

You have records. Genealogy. You have documents.

HARVEY

We have pain too.

DIKRAN

You could just as easily say the Jews brought it on themselves. They're the chosen people. Who said?

HARVEY

So let them have that fantasy. The real question is: why should it bother people to have them think that way? Why not let them have their fun, their illusions? When you go around saying that Jesus is your personal savior, aren't you saying you're chosen too?

DESIREE

Holy Moses, I thought this was a goddamn whorehouse.

HARVEY

People don't know the first thing about me. I may be mulatto but my grandfather was a Nubian. Most people don't even know what a Nubian is. They don't even know there was a Nubian civilization seven thousand years ago. What the hell is a lousy Renaissance a couple a hundred years ago compared to that?

DESIREE

My neighbor had two Nubian goats once.

A new client enters.

DESIREE

Hey! (*She's relieved, hoping the conversation will change*) Hi, cowboy. Merry Christmas.

COWBOY 1

How do, ladies. Merry Christmas to you all. (*Looking at Hyacinth*) Howdy, ma'am. (*He looks at her with a big grin, really taken by her.*)

DESIREE

Hi! Welcome to Zoe's. Out to enjoy yourself, cowboy?

COWBOY 1

Yes ma'am. Always do at Zoe's. 'Smy favorite place on planet earth.

HYACINTH

(*changing stools to be closer to him*) Hi, big fella!

COWBOY 1

Hi. Come here often? That's just a joke, ma'am.

HYACINTH

I come all the time.

COWBOY 1

Oh wow. I like the way that sounds.

HYACINTH

And I make all kinds of sounds too.

COWBOY 1

Oh wow, hey, I think this is somethin we oughta go discuss in private.

HYACINTH

I'm all yours, handsome. (*She takes him by the arm and they leave for one of the back rooms.*)

HARVEY

(*to Dikran, to change the subject*) Show us that picture of your wife.

DIKRAN

Takes out his wallet.

CORAL

(*looking at photograph*) She's a very attractive blond. Doesn't look at all Armenian.

DIKRAN

There's no such thing as a blond Armenian. She's German.

HARVEY

So what the Turks started with the sword you'll finish with the marriage ceremony. You marry out and pretty soon there'll be no Armenians left.

DIKRAN

Well, maybe that's our fate. Maybe we'll all get blended into one group and there'll be peace on earth and mercy mild. We'll all be mulatto like you and then there won't be any race hatred because there won't be any more races.

PHIL

You mean we're all going to look like *him*? Oh God.

DIKRAN

Yeah, you're right! And then the fighting will start between the pale mulattoes and the dark mulattoes.

NICOLE

(*shruggingly*) They all fuck the same.

PHIL

Bad or good?

NICOLE

Jesus. That's all they ever think about. That and how big their shlong is.

HARVEY

What about all the misery my people went through? Does anybody here know what misery is? I mean do you really know what misery is? Misery is pain that *lasts*.

DIKRAN

I'm suffering from Jewish guilt. That's misery.

YITZAKH

Pardon me. I'm a little confused. I thought I was the Jew here.

DIKRAN

You don't have to be Jewish to suffer Jewish guilt. Believe me, the Jews have no monopoly on guilt.

HARVEY

Do you hate the Turks?

DIKRAN

They're people too.

HARVEY

Yeah but do you hate them?

DIKRAN

Why not? They're people like you and me. No, actually I love them.

HARVEY

You *love* them?

DIKRAN

They drove all the Armenians out to America. Imagine living in Turkey if we had stayed! The unhappiness they suffered there!

PHIL

In Hammurabi's time, a woman's chastity was her family's property. Hence honor killings. Blood cleanses honor.

CORAL

Yeah, we need to bring all that back, right? (*It has obviously hit a nerve with her.*) Women who get killed are basically prostitutes, right? That's why we kill them. By we I mean they. It's a cleansing operation, right?

HARVEY

Who gets cleansed?

CORAL

Honor gets cleansed.

                        HARVEY

Yes but the women get killed.

                        YITZAKH

Well, that's the cleansing part.

                        CORAL

(sarcastically) Yeah, collateral damage. Honor and truth are the two most important things in life, right?

                        DAWN

(*mumbles*) And here I thought schwanz was the most important thing in life.

                        HARVEY

What truth? We'll never get to any truth until we know who's making how much money and from what.

                        YITZAKH

How you gonna know that?

                        HARVEY

You follow the money trail.

                        YITZAKH

My money trail led to bankruptcy court. Banks. Banks know who has what. And they're not going to tell you. There are laws.

                        HARVEY

Laws. Laws are made to be changed.

                        PHIL

"Laws grind the poor, and rich men make the laws."

                        CORAL

What?

                        PHIL

(shakes his head sadly) Nothing.

                        YITZAKH

Banks make the laws.

                        HARVEY

Yeah. They're the ones who have all the power. When you have all the wealth you have all the power.

YITZAKH

I thought it was us Jews who had all the wealth – present company excluded.

DIKRAN

The Jews are behind everything, if you ask me.

Suddenly embarrassed by what he has just said as everyone turns and stares at him.

No, I'm just saying.

HARVEY

We need to know what happens behind the scenes. Otherwise we're just fooling ourselves with democracy. Until you know who runs the world you'll never have peace, ya know. Money runs the world.

YITZAKH

There's never going to be peace.

CORAL

Why?

YITZAKH

There's no money in peace.

DIKRAN

Peace. What a novel idea.

YITZAKH

Yeah, we should give it a shot.

DESIREE

Anybody here wanna get laid, by any chance? (*Silence.*) Just a thought.

HARVEY

Just open your eyes. Every country has the same history. It starts out with hopes and aspirations and democracy and ends up with corruption and offshore accounts. Look at America after it wiped out the Indians.

DIKRAN

What about China? It's got all the money in the world.

HARVEY

Right now China is a special case.

DIKRAN

What do you mean?

HARVEY

A good machinery of corruption takes time.

PHIL

Don't kid yourself. The Chinese invented corruption.

YITZAKH

What makes you so cynical?

HARVEY

I'm not cynical. It's the way we're made. I'm only describing human nature.

YITZAKH

So you blame it on God.

HARVEY

Not God. God didn't create banks.

CORAL

First Bank of Jesus Christ.

HARVEY

Right, the ol' Jesus Saves joke.

YITZAKH

All those Jews who were killed by Hitler. How many great authors there would have been among them! How many artists and scientists and statesmen!

CORAL

And bankers. Ah well, that's something nobody'll ever know. The door we didn't go through. Et cetera and so forth.

DIKRAN

The Armenian people were killed in large numbers. (*To Yitzakh*) They got six million of your people. They only got one and a half million of us.

YITZAKH

We should pity you.

DIKRAN

You're lucky. Many Jews got away. Us, they exterminated. They killed only one and a half million of us only because that's all there was at the time.

YITZAKH
They ran out of Armenians.

DIKRAN
Exactly. And we left no record behind. And that's what's most painful of all. The world's silence. It's like saying the events never happened. There wasn't television news coverage in those days or footage you could replay over and over again. So stop complaining.

DESIREE
You know, I really hate to sound old-fashioned about this, but I thought this was a cathouse, not the high-school debating society.

DIKRAN
We can confront the Germans with films, documents made by the Nazis themselves that prevent them from denying anything. But what do the Armenians have? Were they filmed starving to death in the desert?

YITZAKH
Hitler said, "Who remembers the Armenians?"

DIKRAN
That's our claim to fame now.

HARVEY
What is?

DIKRAN
Hitler.

YITZAKH
Hit-ler?

DIKRAN
It's a start.

YITZAKH
Boy, there's nothing new under the moon.

We hear short orgasmic whimpers from one of the bedrooms – not screaming – and everyone is silent to hear it better. Awe, respect, satisfaction.

YITZAKH

Bingo.

Silence.

YITZAKH

It's like those African nations constantly killing each other. Every time you turn around some country has changed its name again. Rand McNally makes a fortune on Africa alone.

DIKRAN

I'm gonna write a book. I'm gonna dedicate it to all those just people who have been maltreated by the unjust.

HARVEY

Dedicated to eight billion people.

NICOLE

And counting.

YITZAKH

Here's your title: "The Rise and Fall."

HARVEY

The Rise and Fall of what?

YITZAKH

Just that. "The Rise and Fall".

HARVEY

Like an erection.

DIKRAN

Your mind is between your legs.

YITZAKH

Can you think of a better place for an erection?

DIKRAN

Dedicate it to orphans. In the past century alone, we created a million orphans. That's a record.

YITZAKH

Call Guinness.

DIKRAN

(*to Dawn*) Does anybody ever try to kiss you?

DAWN

Sometimes.

DIKRAN

Do you let 'em?

DAWN

No. It's the one part of my anatomy I keep the rights to.

DIKRAN

Yeah. That's your *real* private part.

DAWN

You got *that* right. Pussies are practically anonymous.

DIKRAN

But some have more personality than others.

DAWN

I wouldn't go so far as to say that.

DIKRAN

You know, I've always wondered. What's your chief aim in life?

DAWN

My chief aim in life? It's to get through the day.

DIKRAN

We each have different aims, I guess.

DAWN

What's yours?

DIKRAN

I'm still working on it.

NICOLE

The chief aim in this establishment is to guide various male instruments into various female orifices. (*She laughs.*) Joke.

DIKRAN

Vaginally speaking.

NICOLE

Not necessarily.

DIKRAN

Well, hope springs eternal, as Shakespeare once noted.

NICOLE

Who?

DIKRAN

William Shakespeare. The English playwright? He said hope springs eternal.

NICOLE

I once had a friend named Hope Springs. Or wait. I think her name was Hope Summer. Or Summer Hopes.

CORAL

(*to Dawn*) The only thing I don't like about working here is that they try to talk to you. They think they're being nice by treating you as a human being instead of as just a piece of meat. But it only bores you when they do that. You want them to just do the thing and get it over with. What they don't seem to realize is that as far as I'm concerned, I *am* a piece of meat. For them. What do they expect, a woman? They're coming to the wrong place for that.

NICOLE

Yes, and after a while you get sick of people's stories. They're nice people and so on, but you're not their psychiatrist.

DAWN

Yeah, and you know that guy Clark?

CORAL

The one they call Clark Kent?

DAWN

He comes here often since his wife left him. He's a real gentleman in the sack. Sometimes he comes over with that funny golfer friend of his. One afternoon the two of them had Desiree and I twice each in one afternoon. It was like a marathon, or something.

(An old Irishman wanders in. He's here for sentimental reasons. He heard that Zoe's is closing up, and he's devastated. He's here for one last hurrah, as he would put it. He sits disconsolately at the bar. He notices Dawn and brightens up.)

OLD IRISHMAN

Hi.

CRAWFORD

Enters – unnoticed, or so he thinks, because HARVEY sees him.

HARVEY

Hey, you come here too?

CRAWFORD

(caught, laughs uncomfortably) Social visit.

HARVEY

Yeah, well, we're all here on a social visit.

CRAWFORD

Takes it like a sport.

HARVEY

Just hope we don't get any social disease.

CRAWFORD

At Zoe's? Never happened.

OLD IRISHMAN

(He looks at Dawn with a grin of enormous happiness. She gives him a smile back. Working his bushy eyebrows up and down and tilting his head, he indicates the rear of the establishment. He and Dawn leave for one of the back rooms.)

CORAL

Speaking of social diseases, let's get a look at that letter. C'mon!

DESIREE

I know where it is. Follow me. (*DESIREE and CORAL leave by one door as ZOE enters by another.*)

CRAWFORD

(*Sees Zoe and looks at her quietly, admiringly.*)

ZOE

(*to Nicole – she has still not seen Crawford*) Call up the Public Health Center. There's gotta be a mistake. (*Nicole leaves. Zoe turns and sees Crawford.*) Oh shit! What do *you* want?

CRAWFORD

Zoe, I need to talk to you.

ZOE

I have an overwhelming wish not to speak to you.

CRAWFORD

Oh Zoe, give me a break.

ZOE

What are you up to, anyhow?

CRAWFORD

What do you mean, what am I up to? Everything I do is open and aboveboard. I'm not up to anything.

ZOE

Yeah. Mr. Transparency. I can see right through you.

CRAWFORD

Look, I try to be honest.

ZOE

You? Honest? Transparency in human affairs is the only way to get people to be honest, and I see no evidence of it.

CRAWFORD

It's because transparency is a noble but hopeless cause. What's so special about transparency?

ZOE

People like to know how things work. They wanna know what's going on. Who's doing what. It builds trust.

CRAWFORD

Privacy builds trust too.

ZOE

You probably have a private numbered account offshore somewhere.

CRAWFORD

Would I tell you if I did?

ZOE

(*playfully faking it as a temptress*) You'd tell *me*, wouldn't you?

CRAWFORD

If I *had* a numbered account – no. And besides, what's wrong with having secret accounts?

ZOE

Why have secrets? Why do bankers have a need for so much secrecy?

CRAWFORD

Secret is just another name for private. You, you just have a grudge against banks ever since First Farmers of Nevada screwed you out of something.

ZOE

Screwed me out of something? It's you who screwed me out of something – out of a small fortune.

CRAWFORD

Look, I gave you good advice. And I took the same risk and the same advice myself.

ZOE

You call that advice? I call it a shafting.

CRAWFORD

It was my best advice at the time. I have to admit I was in way over my head. I was taken in. I guess I was a little naïve. The big banks in New York sold things that were designed to fail. How could I know that? They bet on them to fail. And the rating agencies gave these made-to-fail products five-star ratings. They sold them to pension funds and municipalities and even whole countries.

ZOE

Yakkity-yak.

CRAWFORD

Nobody could predict the whole market would practically tank.

ZOE

The market didn't tank. The subprime mortgages tanked. Some advice, putting all my cash into some high-risk crap – which made you a bundle, as I recall.

CRAWFORD

When the markets tanked, the big banks scooped up the assets at bargain-basement prices.

ZOE

Yeah yeah yeah, the only thing that didn't fail were the banks. How come the banks didn't fail? Because they were too big to fail and needed government bailout money? Did you ever hear of such crookedness? And the taxpayers, those well-intentioned suckers, came through as they always do. They don't know the crooks they're up against.

CRAWFORD

It was all unpredictable. Everybody was giving the same advice. I'm in it just as deep as you are.

ZOE

So what do you want from me now?

CRAWFORD

Zoe, look, I mean it. I'm really in it just as deep as you are and I've got to pay up what I owe or I'm sunk.

ZOE

Which of course means I have to pay you.

CRAWFORD

Well, I wouldn't put it that bluntly. But yes.

ZOE

You're the financial genius. Maybe you could explain to me how I could pay you when you already have all my money.

CRAWFORD

OK, look. There's this French group in Vegas that wants to buy The House of All Nations.

ZOE

What?!

CRAWFORD

They're willing to pay good money, Zoe. You could retire forever.

ZOE

You mean that Marie Antoinette thing?

CRAWFORD

(*Laughs*) You mean the St. Joan of Arc Consortium.

ZOE

Jesus!

CRAWFORD

Look, I know it sounds –

ZOE

You want the short "no" answer or the long "no" answer?

CRAWFORD

Zoe, they're willing to –

ZOE

They want to *close* this place! You know what? I've heard of that group. They're buying out all the competition. They're becoming a monopoly on pussy.

CRAWFORD

In Vegas? Hardly. They'd have to buy all of Nevada.

ZOE

What makes you think they don't already own all of Nevada. Who owns *them*, by the way?

CRAWFORD

A very solid Swiss bank.

ZOE

A *Swiss* bank? Boy, this is getting creepy. What's their name – Deutschland Ueber Alles?

CRAWFORD

No, that's German. These people are Swiss.

ZOE

But they have a German branch? The Deutsche Bundesbank or something Ueber Alles.

CRAWFORD

Zoe, what are you talking about? Let's get back to reality.

ZOE

You get back to reality! I'm going back to work. This place needs me now more than ever. You shouldn't have gotten me started on banks. Banks and credit cards. They're no better than the Mafia.

CRAWFORD

The Mafia!? (*laughs*)

ZOE

The Mafia charges you six for five, which is about what banks do. Just do the math. Do you know how many people are drowning in debt because of some *schmuck* bank that they thought was helping them?

CRAWFORD

My, what language.

ZOE

Because of some *fuckhead* bank? Do you know how much misery is caused around the world by banks? Why do people have such a high opinion of banks?

CRAWFORD

Well, in an ideal world . . .

ZOE

Fuck an ideal world. We have to work with *this* one.

CRAWFORD

Well, if there are loopholes in the law . . .

ZOE

*Loop*holes? (*incensed*) *Loop*holes? What we need is loopholes for the poor.

CRAWFORD

The poor? All the poor ever want is more. They don't care about consequences. Consequences become real to them only when it threatens their life.

ZOE

Avery, you dumb bastard, the poor want more because they don't have *any*thing. They've got *nada*.

CRAWFORD

You must be getting old.

ZOE

Old, yes, foolish, no. And stupid, definitely not.

CRAWFORD

You're mellowing out is all. You look so lovely, mellowing out.

ZOE

Oh sweet Jesus!

CRAWFORD

Oh hey, let's leave him out of this. (*joking*) Two's company.

ZOE

You know, it's strange, but I might like you more if you had less money.

CRAWFORD

(*to himself*) You may get your wish . . . (*to Zoe*) You *are* getting old. But you'll always be special to me.

ZOE

Look who's mellowing out.

CRAWFORD

But you *know* I love you. I've loved you all along.

ZOE

The last of the romantics.

CRAWFORD

Don't my actions speak louder than words?

ZOE

They sure do.

CRAWFORD

What do you want from me?

ZOE

Nothing.

CRAWFORD

I let you down, didn't I?

ZOE

No, you attacked me.

CRAWFORD

Attacked you – how?

ZOE

By throwing my money away and leaving me exposed to this – to this buy-out thing. Not to mention exposed to a bunch of crazy puritans. The Family That Lays Together Stays Together.

CRAWFORD

It's the Family Above All.

ZOE

Right. The Family Ueber Alles.

CRAWFORD

But they're just a bunch of little old ladies.

ZOE

That's the trouble. They're a bunch of little old ladies. Plus little old Mayor Brinkerhoff, who's another little old lady. Plus every blue nose in a county that has more blue noses than there's tumbleweed.

CRAWFORD

Do you think anyone has the power to stop a morals squad?

ZOE

I know you don't have the power. You have the power only to grab land and send money to Switzerland. Or is it the Caymans this week?

CRAWFORD

Are you mad? Where do you think I get money from? As a banker I have a salary, like everybody else.

ZOE

Sure, and everybody drives around in a Mercedes too and gets a million-dollar Christmas bonus.

CRAWFORD

You would think I was a billionaire, the way you talk.

ZOE

(makes a huge whooping sound)

CRAWFORD

I wouldn't want a nice friendly place like this to close down. It makes everybody happy. I like this place. Everybody likes this place.

ZOE

Except the old biddies in town – of both sexes. Now beat it. I've got work to do.

(She leaves. Crawford, at a loss, looks around and, reluctantly, is about to leave, as Phil comes over.)

PHIL

Hey, J. P. Morgan! Where's darling beloved?

CRAWFORD

I think I was just dismissed by her.

PHIL

You know what I would do if I were in your shoes and had just been dismissed by Zoe?

CRAWFORD

What would you do?

PHIL

I'd leave, vamoose. I would disappear and be gone. I'd never be seen again.

CRAWFORD

Phil, we've known each other a long time. Maybe you could help me with a little problem.

PHIL

I'll be honest with you. Little problems baffle me. Now if I had a big problem to work with . . .

CRAWFORD

This is a big problem. You know I don't want this place to close down any more than you do.

PHIL

Yeah, I know, that's how the world works. People are always being forced to do what they don't want to do. Funny how it's always the ones with money expressing the regret, and it's always the ones without money who regretfully lose out. I wonder who regrets more.

CRAWFORD

You too? Look, Phil, that's so unfair.

PHIL

Precisely what the poor keep saying.

CRAWFORD

Oh, what's the use. I get it. I'm leaving.

>*Crawford exits. Shortly thereafter Mayor Stanley Brinkerhoff wanders in, looking a little lost.*

PHIL

What are you doing here? This isn't Tuesday.

BRINKERHOFF

Not so loud. I have to talk to Zoe.

PHIL

You too?

BRINKERHOFF

What do you mean, me too?

PHIL

Your ole buddy was just here. The Great Crawford.

BRINKERHOFF

Hunt was just here? I thought his day was Fridays. I thought we had worked out that –

PHIL

He was just here to see Zoe. But he wanted to see her in a big way.

BRINKERHOFF

I guess it's all beginning to fall apart, isn't it. The dreaded event. Is she around?

PHIL

It all depends on what you want to see her for.

BRINKERHOFF

Well, you know the pressure is on.

PHIL

What pressure?

                              BRINKERHOFF
You know, the pressure.

                                  PHIL
You mean you.

                              BRINKERHOFF
Me?

                                  PHIL
You're the pressure.

                              BRINKERHOFF
Well, it's them old biddies, it's not me After all they're an important part of my
constituency. As elected mayor of our beautiful town, this portion of God's green
Nevada that we're so fortunate to inhabit, I'm here to serve everyone. Biddies
included.

                    *Nicole, busy behind the bar, overhears the last bit
                    of dialogue.*

                                NICOLE
Yes, but you don't have to kowtow to them.

                              BRINKERHOFF
Well, they're pretty angry. And frankly, you know . . .

                                NICOLE
Yeah, I know. Frankly they vote.

                              BRINKERHOFF
Well, you can't just ignore them. What would you like me to do?

                                NICOLE
Piss on them.

                              BRINKERHOFF
(*bridles*) You can't piss on them. (*With sudden civic stirrings*) They're people!

                                NICOLE
You mean they're voters.

                              BRINKERHOFF
Well, yes, I grant you they're voters, but you can't just go around pissing on voters.

NICOLE

(with *sweet cynicism*) Oh no? You must be out to rewrite the whole of Western history. What do politicians do except piss on people?

BRINKERHOFF

Nicole, give me a break. Their point of view must be respected too.

NICOLE

The only one who can give you a break around here is Zoe. If you're lucky.

BRINKERHOFF

Oh Zoe will help me out. We've been friends a long time.

Desiree passes through.

DESIREE

(*in a teasing singsong as she passes by him*) Hi, Stanley!

BRINKERHOFF

(*embarrassed*) Oh, uh – (*quietly*) oh hello, Desiree.

DESIREE

How they hanging?

She leaves.

NICOLE

What point do they have?

BRINKERHOFF

What? (*His mind is still on Desiree.*) What?

NICOLE

The biddies. You said their point of view must be respected. So what's their point of view?

BRINKERHOFF

(*recovering*) Well, they have an understandable concern. You know, our children. In our little town to have an establishment of – well, of this sort – sends the wrong message to kids growing up here. You know, morals and all that. It's a part of our function, you know, as the elders of the town, to set them a good example toward the straight and narrow path and, you know, the good life.

NICOLE

Can it. You've already been elected mayor.

BRINKERHOFF

Do you have kids?

NICOLE

Me? No, thank God. I couldn't do that to another human being. Bring a kid into *this* world?

PHIL

Pretty shitty.

NICOLE

Pretty shitty.

PHIL

This meshugana world.

NICOLE

I didn't know you were Jewish.

PHIL

We're all Jewish. The whole world's Jewish.

NICOLE

My biggest dream is to have a better life.

PHIL

What is a better life?

BRINKERHOFF

Still, you've got a happy little family here, no?

NICOLE

As happy as it gets, I suppose.

PHIL

Considering some of the men we get here. Some of them are one chromosome away from a turnip.

NICOLE

On good days, you mean. We had one guy here yesterday who was missing that chromosome. He even looked like a turnip.

PHIL

All families are happy now.

NICOLE

What do you mean?

PHIL

There's no more unhappiness now. Got a problem? The drug companies give it a name and tell you there's no need to suffer. They have a pill for it and presto! You do feel better. So now all unhappy families are alike too.

BRINKERHOFF

If I can't see Zoe I've got to get back to my office. I can't be seen here during work hours. It would give a bad impression. This is terrible, this is terrible, I've gotta go.

PHIL

And no more talk of closing down. The whole town would go into mourning.

BRINKERHOFF

It's not me. I'm all for keeping things as they are, you know me.

PHIL

Everybody here knows you. Even better than your wife knows you.

HYACINTH

(*coming back*) Oh hi, your honor.

BRINKERHOFF

(*flustered*) Hi – uh –

HYACINTH

Hyacinth.

BRINKERHOFF

Yeah, Hyacinth.

> *Brinkerhoff leaves by one door as CORAL comes in by another.*

CORAL

(*sniffing the air*) I know that aftershave. Old teeny dick's been here.)

HYACINTH

Oh he's OK. He's just not a shower – he's a grower.

CORAL

Unlike Avery. Ave's got a schwanz and a half.

HYACINTH

Sometimes I think that's why Zoe loves him.

CORAL

She's crazy to go for Crawford.

HYACINTH

Because of the schwanz or in spite of the schwanz?

CORAL

He's a crook. He's not an honest man.

HYACINTH

Since when did that ever stop love?

CORAL

She deserves better.

HYACINTH

Who doesn't deserve better? She should talk to –

She's interrupted as two men come in.

HYACINTH

– oh, howdy, cowboys, a Merry Christmas to y'all.

COWBOY 2

How'do, ladies. A little nippy out there.

HYACINTH

Well, come on in. We've got just what's needed to warm you up.

CORAL

Nice day for it too, don't you think?

COWBOY 3

(*looking her up and down*) Sure looks nice from here.

COWBOY 2

Heard you were closing and didn't want to miss out.

CORAL

Vicious rumor. If you're looking for a good time you've come to the right place.

(*In talking with the cowboys CORAL and HYACINTH have lapsed into a cowboy drawl.*)

COWBOY 2

I'd wonder why anybody would want to close down a nice place like this, all friendly like. It sure makes everybody happy.

CORAL

Hey, handsome, don't let it worry you. It aint gonna happen. It's just a little political game that gets played every election year.

HYACINTH

When you run for office, you shut down the whorehouse. That way we all get a little rest, the mayor gets reelected and then we open up again.

COWBOY 3

Hey, where's Stardust? Ain't she working today?

NICOLE

It's her day off today. She's at her other job.

COWBOY 3

What job is that?

NICOLE

In Vegas. She does therapy on the side. Her specialty is compulsive gambling and she also does a little marital counseling on the side. You know, helps out people with marital problems.

COWBOY 2

You're joking.

NICOLE

I'm serious. She's studying clinical psychology. Or *was* studying clinical psychology. She always wanted to be a psychologist but was also drawn to self-degradation, so there was a conflict right there.

COWBOY 2

Wow, only in Vegas.

PHIL

I wouldn't laugh. She's very good at what she does.

COWBOY 3

Which? Working here? Or helping people with marital problems?

PHIL

There really ain't much difference between the two.

COWBOY 3

Who's all working today? Kinda looking forward to an early Christmas present to myself.

CORAL

Well, we're your gifts, big fella.

HYACINTH

All ready to be unwrapped.

CORAL

(*coyly*) Yeah, cowboy, hope you like what's in the box.

HYACINTH

Hope you're not too disappointed.

COWBOY 3

Hell no, ma'am!

CORAL

Like your enthusiasm, Cowboy.

COWBOY 3

Ah'm told s'mah biggest quality. Second only to ridin a bronco.

HYACINTH

Do you ride anything besides broncos?

COWBOY 3

What d'jave in mind?

HYACINTH

Like do a little saddlin up and goin for a pony ride?

COWBOY 2

Sounds good to me. (*Entering into the game.*) If it's not too personal, ah've always wanted to peek into a girl's tack room.

CORAL

Su casa, big fella. My tack room's yours – poke around and see if there's anything you'd like. (*Flaunting her breasts.*) You might even find a pair of stirrup cups you like.

COWBOY 2

Those're mighty high up for stirrup cups.

COWBOY 3

They must be Victoria's Secret stirrup cups.

CORAL

Nuthin there that ain't natural, big fella.

HYACINTH

You boys have come to the right place.

COWBOY 3

(eagerly) Oh I know that, ma'am! I know that!

HYACINTH

Mmmm. (with sympathy) Been a while for you, hasn't it.

COWBOY 3

Not since the last time, ma'am.

She links arms with him in a friendly way, jamming a breast affectionately into his upper arm as she steers him around like an old chum. All four leave with smiles that anticipate an afternoon's fun. HYACINTH comments as they leave:

HYACINTH

Well, cowboy, we'll make up for lost time. You boys just got yourself here two mares ready for hitchin.

For a moment the room is empty except for Phil and Nicole and the regulars at the bar. On the silent stage a middle-aged dowdily-dressed woman appears, coming in quietly and looking around timidly about being in a house of prostitution.

PHIL

Can I help you?

MRS. LITTLEFIELD

(*startled and suddenly switching to an arrogant act*) Who, may I ask, are you?

PHIL

A fellow sufferer in life. And may I in turn inquire as to your identity or, if you prefer, moniker?

MRS. LITTLEFIELD

You may inquire. But it seems to me that if you're suffering in life, you shouldn't be in a place like this.

PHIL

A place like this?

MRS. LITTLEFIELD

Come off it. You know exactly what I mean. Mme. Zoe's place. (*Pause before distastefully adding:*) Whorehouse.

PHIL

Ah! The House of All Nations!

MRS. LITTLEFIELD

No – a *whore*house of all nations! A place of vice and sin. Of fornication. A blight on earth and cesspool of immorality. A descent into vulgar unspeakability –

PHIL

Whoa, hold on, whoa, stop! You should be ashamed of yourself for even entering a place like that.

MRS. LITTLEFIELD

Don't mock me, you – you – who *are* you, anyway?

PHIL

Depends. Are you from the IRS?

MRS. LITTLEFIELD

Don't be ridiculous!

PHIL

No, I can see you're not. I work here in the august capacity of bouncer. My function in life is to keep out undesirables – unceremoniously bounce them out, as it were. And now, madame, having completed the very pleasant social obligation of introducing myself to you, who, may I ask, are you?

MRS. LITTLEFIELD

Where is she?

PHIL

Ah, you have come back to the embraces of an old flame of yours, and on Christmas Eve. How touching! You have come for a sentimental reunion with – . Which "she" did you mean? There are several "she's working here.

                    MRS. LITTLEFIELD
Don't be repulsive.

                    PHIL
Well, I'm doing my best. Where is who, then?

                    MRS. LITTLEFIELD
Mme. Zoe. Or is she one of the undesirables that you've so unceremoniously bounced?

                    PHIL
Before I answer, I hope you won't think I was blowing your cover if I were to ask if you're from the Family Above All?

                    MRS. LITTLEFIELD
That *is* my affiliation.

                    PHIL
Ah. You look it, too.

                    MRS. LITTLEFIELD
And it is not a cover, as you call it. I'm proud to be a member of our association. I demand to see Mme. Zoe.

                    PHIL
On the part of Mrs. – ?

                    MRS. LITTLEFIELD
Mrs. Littlefield – of the First Farmers of Nevada.

                    PHIL
Mrs. Little–

                    MRS. LITTLEFIELD
–field.

                    PHIL
Lady, in your shoes, I wouldn't be in a rush to demand *any*thing of Mme. Zoe. Out of a desire to protect you, I will soften your communication to a respectful request for a moment of her time. In other words, don't push your luck.

                           MRS. LITTLEFIELD
If it's not too much trouble.

                           PHIL
No trouble, I think I can safely assure you that. Something tells me she will be
happy to see you. I've heard her express a small degree of curiosity about the
Family Above All.

                           MRS. LITTLEFIELD
Hmpf!

                                        *Phil leaves. In his absence, Mrs. Littlefield sniffs
                                        around the bar, finding the setting generally
                                        offensive, causing her to react with distaste.
                                        Yitzakh and Dikran at the bar track her
                                        movements with interest but say nothing. Less
                                        than a minute or so passes and then Phil returns
                                        with Zoe.*

                           ZOE
Mrs. Littlefield?

                           MRS. LITTLEFIELD
Yes. You're – ?

                           ZOE
Zoe Muhlbach, ay-kay-ay Mme. Zoe to friends and the Wicked Witch of the West
to others.

                           MRS. LITTLEFIELD
I come to you as a representative of the Family Above All.

                           ZOE
Yes, your cross to bear. And how may I do you?

                           MRS. LITTLEFIELD
By now I'm sure you've heard of us.

                           ZOE
I recall the occasional squib in the back pages of the local rag.

MRS. LITTLEFIELD

Please. I don't like game playing. As you well know, we're shutting you down by order of Mr. Stanley Brinkerhoff and I'm here –

ZOE

You mean Old Stan . . . (*beginning to say something about him but recovering*) Oh, yes, Stanley Brinkerhoff, the mayor.

MRS. LITTLEFIELD

An upright member of our community.

ZOE

He's often upright here. Sometimes a small problem of his comes up – a very small one, I might add – but he never goes away unsatisfied. Mrs. Littleton, let's cut to the chase and save us both a lot of wasted breath.

MRS. LITTLEFIELD

Field.

ZOE

What?

MRS. LITTLEFIELD

Field. Little-*field*. Not Littleton.

ZOE

We're not closing, and it doesn't matter a rat's ass what Stanley Brinkerhoff thinks.

MRS. LITTLEFIELD

Oh but you are so wrong. He has the force of the law behind him. And the law is clear. By local ordinance authorized under Proposition 42, this establishment must have its doors closed by six p.m., which leaves you (*peers down at her lapel watch*) exactly two hours and fifty-five minutes to comply with the law. Mr. Brinkerhoff is prepared to put a police lock on your outside gate at that hour, and I can assure you of his eagerness to do so. Several deputies will be posted to see that all goes smoothly and without hiccup. I think I make myself clear?

ZOE

And how is Mr. Littlewheel?

MRS. LITTLEFIELD

–field.

ZOE

Whatever.

MRS. LITTLEFIELD

Mr. Littlefield is no concern of yours.

ZOE

It was just a matter of solicitude. You seem so on edge I couldn't help wondering if you were getting any lately.

MRS. LITTLEFIELD

I find you offensive and insulting. Especially in view of the fact that my poor dear husband is no longer here.

ZOE

Disappeared, has he? Just took off?

MRS. LITTLEFIELD

He just recently died.

ZOE

Oh, sorry to hear that. But I wonder if you've ever examined your homoerotic tendencies, because there's always that way out in one's lonely advancing years. A little companionship on winter nights, with perhaps a little brandy before a crackling fire.

MRS. LITTLEFIELD

How *dare* you!

ZOE

There's nothing wrong with a little lezzy love – you know, two little old ladies being all cuddly in a nice warm bed drinking hot chocky? The picture is so pretty.

MRS. LITTLEFIELD

Ugh!

ZOE

Ah, you're fighting it, Mrs. Littlebit, you're fighting it.

MRS. LITTLEFIELD

This is too much!

ZOE

Out here women sometimes outnumber men two to one, and our desert nights do get cold. And we women are *so* much more loving than men, don't you think? – and so much more wonderfully needy, if you know what I mean.

MRS. LITTLEFIELD

Delude yourself all you want. I'm leaving. But not before telling you that your manipulations of Mr. Avery Crawford will do you no good.

ZOE

Good God, woman, I have no idea what you're talking about.

MRS. LITTLEFIELD

Did you know his nephew has been arrested?

ZOE

Hunt?

MRS. LITTLEFIELD

Yes, Huntington. Dear Mr. Crawford's nephew.

ZOE

Nephew-in-law.

MRS. LITTLEFIELD

Hunt, as you call him.

ZOE

Arrested for what?

MRS. LITTLEFIELD

Possession.

ZOE

Of drugs?

MRS. LITTLEFIELD

Possession and *sale*. Of course of drugs. What did you think I meant – *hot chocky*? He's been selling to one of your young ladies.

ZOE

That can't be true! That's an utter lie!

MRS. LITTLEFIELD

Oh I'm afraid not, Mrs. Zoe. Ah-ha, I see I have you worried! He can be reached at the – how would you phrase it? – at the local hoosegow. And so you see, the authorities have what is known, I believe, as the goods on you. Yours may be a modest little enterprise but in the eyes of the law that is of no consequence. It's never size that matters –

ZOE

Oh I agree with you there.

MRS. LITTLEFIELD

– but illicitness of activity. And drugs are a no-no. In short, I'm happy to say your little operation here will soon be a memory.

ZOE

Who did he sell to?

MRS. LITTLEFIELD

To a young lady who goes, I believe, by the name of Nanette – shortened no doubt from Yes! *Yes*! Nanette.

ZOE

(*laughs, relieved*) Oh for a moment you had me worried.

MRS. LITTLEFIELD

I beg your pardon?

ZOE

Poor Nanette. She left us months ago. She hasn't worked here in ages. You'll probably find her in Vegas somewhere, an independent entrepreneur working hotel lobbies along the Strip. And rather successfully too, I understand, after a cozy arrangement with the local gendarmerie.

MRS. LITTLEFIELD

I don't believe you.

ZOE

Call the police, then, stage a raid on us. It will make for superb publicity, especially when it comes out that you've made a fool of yourself.

MRS. LITTLEFIELD

You're bluffing. Oh, there's no use talking to a person of your kind.

ZOE

Call my bluff, Mrs. Littleheel.

MRS. LITTLEFIELD

(*Hurls over her shoulder as she leaves.*) Don't think I won't! Oh!

Zoe returns to her office.

Dawn has meanwhile come back from her brief old Irish romance (alone) and goes right to work:

DAWN

(*going to the bar and taking a stool next to Dikran*) Hi, cowboy. Where you from?

DIKRAN

I'm not a cowboy and I'm still from Fresno. East Fresno. Haven't moved since I came in.

DAWN

Looking for a good time? I'm all wound up and in the mood for it myself. Let's have some fun.

DIKRAN

No.

DAWN

A little cheerful tete-a-tete? Just between you and I?

DIKRAN

No.

DAWN

I could be nice to you. Don't you like me?

DIKRAN

No.

DAWN

Are you gay?

DIKRAN

No.

DAWN

What brings you to Mme. Zoe's? Oh I get it. Interested in a little voyeurism maybe? We have a special arrangement in Room Number 3.

DIKRAN

No.

DAWN

No. Everything is no with you. You do speak English, don't you?

DIKRAN

No.

DAWN

'Ts what I thought. (*sotto voce* to Nicole) What's with this guy? Does he have a war injury or something?

NICOLE

Oh he's all right. He just needs to be alone.

DAWN

Why?

NICOLE

His wife ran out on him with a lion tamer. He's inconsolable.

DIKRAN

(*hearing them*) I'm not inconsolable. Armenians just look that way.

DAWN

Oh inconsolable! (*sweetly and with genuine feeling*) Oh really, that is *so* –! His wife left him and he's inconsolable! That is *so* touching.

NICOLE

(*looking at her strangely*) Yeah, well, *it* may be touching but don't touch *him*. The guy's just not normal.

Dawn moves down the bar.

DIKRAN

(*to Nicole*) So you're going out of business.

NICOLE

Hey! That's just a rumor. Stop spreading it around. It's not true.

DAWN

People think whorehouses are driven out of business, but they're not. Whorehouses go on forever.

DIKRAN

Do you believe that?

NICOLE

Of course. It's human nature.

DIKRAN

Human nature. Human nature (*quietly, mulling that over*). Everything screwy or illegal turns out to be human nature.

CORAL reappears, alone.

NICOLE

(*to Coral*) Where's Hyacinth?

CORAL

She's still in there with the cowboys. They said they needed privacy for this one. They said they thought up something totally new.

NICOLE

In a whorehouse? There's nothing new in a whorehouse.

DIKRAN

(*turning to Coral*) What would you do if this place closed down?

CORAL

Me? Go to Acapulco. You should see the beaches.

DIKRAN

Got money?

CORAL

In the bank.

DIKRAN

And then?

CORAL

Come back, start working again. There's always a demand for pussy. Prostitution is as inevitable as – as –

DIKRAN

As earwax.

DAWN

It's what makes the world go round.

NICOLE

(*looking around*) The world's not exactly spinning at the moment. Slow day on the old ranch.

PHIL

Well, you know, Christmas Eve.

NICOLE

I'm hungry. I think I'll go make myself a ham sandwich.

(But she doesn't leave.)

NICOLE

Remember old Madeleine?

PHIL

Funny I was just thinking about her. There's a clip here in the paper. Died in her sleep on Christmas Eve.

NICOLE

(in a reminiscent mood) She was 107 years old.

PHIL

Yeah, it says she was 107! Can you believe that? Death was attributed to unknown causes. Which is very funny. A hundred and seven and died of unknown causes.

NICOLE

She used to eat a lot of raw spinach.

PHIL

On white toast, wasn't it?

DAWN

Yeah, you have to balance it out. You know, the way the sugar in a diet Coke and a candy bar cancel each other out? Y'know what I'm driving at?

Yitzakh comes in.

YITZAKH

The bathroom here is like the ones they have in those luxury hotels on the Strip. You know, the MGM type places.

NICOLE

Nothing but the best at Mme. Zoe's.

YITZAKH

It felt like I was using that urinal for the first time.

PHIL

Actually you were. It was a new Parisian urinal the plumber installed yesterday.

YITZAKH

What makes a urinal Parisian? A urinal's a urinal. I mean it's just a porcelain target that you point your percy at. But you know, I got to thinking while I was in there.

PHIL

Whenever I piss at a French urinal I think.

NICOLE

Therefore you are.

PHIL

What?

NICOLE

You *think*, therefore you – never mind.

YITZAKH

I was thinking about bank secrecy. You know what that is? I just realized what bank secrecy is. Bank secrecy is a protection scheme for crooks, that's all it is.

Silence.

NICOLE

I heard our little town of Acacia is trying to get twinned with the town of Pussy in France.

PHIL

There's a town in France called Pussy?

NICOLE

There's pussy in every town in France.

More silence. A gloomy feeling.

NICOLE

(*to get talk going again*) So are you saying Swiss banks are crooks?

More silence. YITZAKH is somewhere far away in his dreams when he speaks again.

YITZAKH

(*almost in a reverie*) They're the biggest crooks in the world. You want to know what's happening in the world? Follow the money. If you open up all the bank accounts in Switzerland and the Cayman Islands you'll get transparency. Illegal money legally held. (*He pauses, struck by his own phrase.*) Yes, illegal money legally held. Top secret accounts. Dictators and billionaires and trillionaires. That would give you more information about what's happening in the world than the evening news ever will. I bet future historians would love to learn these things about us. (*Pause.*) Ten trillion dollars in offshore accounts. Who knows? Maybe a hundred trillion.

> *They all listen to him in a desultory way. There's nothing else to do during this lull in business. But his dismal soliloquy holds little interest for them. YITZAKH, oblivious of their indifference, goes on, speaking to himself.*

YITZAKH

We can no longer live the way we've been doing. We don't even have room left to dump our daily garbage any more, not even at sea. Pollution poisons the planet. The ocean levels are rising and at the same time the rivers are drying up. The ozone layer is shrinking. Gangsters rule our countries . . . . They're not even gangsters anymore. They're banksters now. Same thing . . . it's all the same thing. . . . What did you think it was?

Silence.

NICOLE

Profound thoughts.

PHIL

You thought all this at the urinal? You should piss more often. There's still the whole Middle East to work out.

Silence again. Then:

DAWN

I've been thinking of doing sex work for the CIA.

PHIL

Sex work for the CIA. Without wishing to be overly inquisitive or in any sense pushy, what exactly does the CIA do in the way of sex work?

DAWN

You know, instead of torture. You get criminals in a nice comfortable bed and get all cozy with them and they open up and start talking. That way you get them all interrogated and debriefed.

PHIL

You don't debrief criminals. You debrief our side. Unless you're talking about removing the gentleman's briefs.

DAWN

It would certainly be easier to do sex work if you removed the guy's briefs, doncha think?

PHIL

You got a point there.

DAWN

I mean, it's a good idea, doncha think?

PHIL

It's an idea whose time has come.

DAWN

It would be the end of the CIA as we know it.

PHIL

It doesn't get better than that.

DIKRAN

(*disgusted*) Yaa! You put the CIA down until you need it.

DAWN

You think I should write to the President and let him know where I'm going with this?

PHIL

I think I'd hold off a while.

> *Desiree, Dawn, and Coral at the bar, joining Dikran, Harvey and Yitzakh, and a glum NICOLE looks at them, then silently looks at her watch.*

DIKRAN

(*studying Desiree*) You know, you have Armenian eyes.

DESIREE

I do? You sure they're not Jewish. Or Irish.

DIKRAN

No, I know Armenian eyes.

DESIREE

I've never been told that before.

DIKRAN

(*looking at her with interest*) Yeah . . . really beautiful . . .

DESIREE

Boys used to tell me I had almond eyes. They used to feel me up a lot. Enjoyed it too – if I liked the guy.

A silence falls on them.

CORAL

Sure looks like we're closing. (*meditatively*) I remember when Viagra first appeared, business went up 20 percent. And now . . .

NICOLE

(*She looks around some more, then suddenly complains loudly*) Jesus, I mean, what kind of Christmas is this, all of us just sitting here? Doesn't anybody want to get laid anymore?

HARVEY

(*shooting his hand up*) Yo!

CURTAIN

ACT II

Lounge bar. With a slight time lapse, action continues from Act I. Dawn, Coral, Desiree and Hyacinth are seated at the bar. Nicole is not there. Harvey occupies a stool in the middle of the bar next to Yitzakh. Phil is as always seated at the end of the bar. He's reading a newspaper. Dikran, at the other end of the bar, sits with his elbows on the bar, his head in his hands, totally out of it, as though in despair.

PHIL

Hey, listen to this. Knuckles Nardelli found dead on Canal Street. Two bullets in the head.

CORAL

Well, he's out of it now. He always wanted to quit the mob.

PHIL

Yeah, he tried to quit two years ago but they wouldn't let him.

CORAL

Why?

PHIL

He was the best hit man they ever had.

CORAL

Why'd he wanna quit?

PHIL

How do I know? Maybe they had a lousy pension plan.

The door bursts open.

TULLY

(storms in with a tall provocatively dressed Las Vegas escort on each arm, shouting in a holiday spirit) Hey, wake up, everybody! Santa's here! It's the goddamned season to be jolly! Wake up, wake up!

CORAL

Look, it's Jack! Jack's here!

ZOE

Jack Tully!

TULLY

None other, ladies, none other. Hey! Whose funeral we attending? Just hope he died in the saddle. Come on, girls, it's the solstice. Start the year off with a bang – get it? (*In a terrible baritone through which words can be made out he launches into:*) "If winter comes can spring be far behind? Come, my sweetheart, let's fondle your behind.")

> *The girls spring to life, genuinely glad to see Tully. They crowd round him in a celebratory mood.*

TULLY

Hey, where's Stardust? – the girl with those wonderful thighs.

DAWN

The girl with the million-dollar legs – and that was before inflation.

CORAL

Stardust's in Vegas. She's at her other job.

TULLY

Too bad, too bad, just when we need her.

HYACINTH

Hey, what about us?

> *Tully grabs Hyacinth and showers her with kisses and hugs and then puts paternal arms around the two escorts he had arrived with and leads them and Hyacinth, Coral, Desiree and Dawn to the back rooms.*

PHIL

Hey, somebody has to hold the fort. What if a client walks in?

DESIREE

(*she drops out*) I don't mind. I could use a break. (*She sits at the bar.*)

PHIL

(*to Tully*) Sure you have enough there.

TULLY

I could always come back for more. Onward to pleasure! Let joy be unconfined!

DAWN

Yeah, onward unconfined. Whatever.

> *At that moment Malcolm comes rushing in, agitated. Tully and the women leave through the other door.*

MALCOLM

Oh uh . . . where's Nicole?

PHIL

Ah the eternal search for the bluebird of happiness.

MALCOLM

(*naively*) We got bluebirds in Nevada now? Wow! Let's get to that next. First where's Nicole.

PHIL

She's gone in search of lemons, no doubt to give life more zest.

PHIL

Oh.

PHIL

I'm sure you understand that nothing occurs at random, but everything happens for a reason and by necessity.

MALCOLM

(*dryly*) You don't say.

PHIL

Aristotle. Actually it was Anaxagoras' view but it was Aristotle who summarized it, though he was talking about ethical behavior and not just citrus fruits.

MALCOLM

I see.

PHIL

However I wouldn't go so far as to say that Aristotle was incapable of original thought.

MALCOLM

Excuse me, clue me in. What are we discussing here?

PHIL

Anaxagoras. He was not in accord with Democritus' atomic theory.

MALCOLM

(*Thinking Phil is joking, he gets into the spirit of it.*) Yeah, you keep hearing that in Vegas.

PHIL

And then it became all quantum.

MALCOLM

A quantum leap, yeah.

PHIL

These were just attempts at learning what the world is. First we imagine something we *think* is the world. Then we call our imaginings our *understanding* of the world. And then we say our understanding *is* the world. Get it?

MALCOLM

Sure. Makes sense. Hey, Phil. Mind me asking how come you work here? I mean, like, what do you do?

PHIL

I bounce. There's an old Hindu saying that it's better to go to a brothel and have your mind on God than go to the temple and have your mind on a brothel.

MALCOLM

(*reasonably*) I see. Did you ever think of getting laid yourself? – you know, surrounded by all this pulchritude, get your ashes hauled?

PHIL

I keep myself pure for my wife.

MALCOLM

I was told your wife is dead.

PHIL

So?

MALCOLM

OK, OK. (*Backing away, conceding.*) Just asking.

PHIL

And please don't tell me it's sad. There's nothing more beautiful than the desert. The desert reminds me of my wife. The desert is as pure as she was.

MALCOLM

Yeah. (*Unconvinced.*) Yeah.

PHIL

You know how us men get without women. You know, we go a little soft in the head after a while.

MALCOLM

Yeah, without women, I get a little soft in the head too. Sometimes a little hard too.

> *Harvey gestures for Malcolm to come over. Phil goes back to reading his newspaper.*

HARVEY

Without being rude, getting hard is what it's all about here.

MALCOLM

(*getting the pun and feeling embarrassed*) Oh, that's not why I'm here.

HARVEY

It's OK, that's the reason I'm here too, so don't think I'm judging you.

MALCOLM

No, seriously, I'm here because –

HARVEY

Oh, hey, right! Sorry! I remember you from before. You're that guy who was talking to Nicole earlier. You had news or something.

MALCOLM

Right, that was me. That is, I still am . . . me.

HARVEY

You like Nicole?

MALCOLM

Oh, uh, well yes, I do kind of like her actually. But I'm here to correct something I screwed up before.

HARVEY

I know just what you mean, we don't often get a chance to go back and correct mistakes we made in life.

MALCOLM

Yeah, I really screwed up before. I guess you must have overheard what it was about. But don't worry, everything will be fine now.

HARVEY

I know it will, buddy, and I'm here to help you. Let me see. You made the wrong impression and now you want to set things straight, right? I think I know how you should proceed.

MALCOLM

I just need to find Nicole and tell her.

HARVEY

I like your determination, but I'm not sure that's the right approach to take.

MALCOLM

It isn't? Wouldn't she want to know right away? I mean, it's good news!

HARVEY

It's good news for you both, but you don't want to become like a bull and just go charging in and overwhelm the girl.

MALCOLM

Bull? What bull?

HARVEY

You! You're ready to declare yourself to Nicole without preparing her for it. How do you think she'll react? You don't want to just plunge in. You want to do it more smoothly.

MALCOLM

(*confused – unaware they're talking at cross purposes*) I mean, you think it'll shock her or something?

HARVEY

It might. After all, you just met her.

MALCOLM

Oh, I wouldn't want to shock her. I already feel bad enough about what I said earlier.

HARVEY

Don't be so self-critical. Take things nice and slow and first get into a conversation with her and then tell her.

MALCOLM

You think? Seems a bit unnecessary. But as long as I tell her in the end I guess it's fine.

HARVEY

That's the spirit. Here she comes. Go to it, tiger – nice and slow.

> *Harvey, a neutral observer now, turns back half-facing the bar as Nicole enters.*

NICOLE

Well if it isn't you!

MALCOLM

Yes, ma'am, it isn't. I mean it is. Me.

NICOLE

Oh don't call me ma'am. Sounds almost immoral. Call me Nicole. They used to call me Knickers in school. So embarrassing. I prefer Nicole.

MALCOLM

Why Knickers?

NICOLE

It's a British thing.

MALCOLM

I prefer Nicole too.

NICOLE

And you're?

MALCOLM

Malcolm. Named after an uncle who went to India.

NICOLE

How fascinating. What did this uncle do in India?

MALCOLM

He fought for their independence.

NICOLE

Oh how noble!

MALCOLM

Yeah. And then shot himself.

NICOLE

Why?

MALCOLM

It's when they assassinated Gandhi – after putting in all those years of work he just lost hope when they assassinated Gandhi.

NICOLE

Poor man.

MALCOLM

Yeah. He was very young and it left his new wife a bereaved widow and quite sad. She could have got together with Phil.

NICOLE

Not Phil. He likes being alone in the desert.

MALCOLM

Is he crazy?

NICOLE

Nah.

MALCOLM

Because I hate to say this but he sounds crazy.

NICOLE

He's a good bouncer. And he's Zoe's cousin and this is the only employment he can get ever since a horse kicked him in the head. He says things like the whole world's a whorehouse, but that doesn't sound too crazy to me. What brings you back here?

MALCOLM

Oh the report. Remember that report I gave you?

NICOLE

The clinic tests. What about them?

MALCOLM

I'm really a little embarrassed to say.

NICOLE

Embarrassed to say what?

MALCOLM

I gave you the wrong report.

NICOLE

What?! Don't be embarrassed. That could be good news – depending.

MALCOLM

I'm not supposed to reveal what it says – but (*looks around conspiratorially*) everybody here is clean as a whistle.

NICOLE

Wow! Wait till I tell Zoe!

MALCOLM

Wait. I have the report with me. The correct one. Here.

NICOLE

We always get a clean report.

MALCOLM

I didn't see your name on the report.

NICOLE

That's because I'm not one of the girls. I just work the bar.

MALCOLM

Oh, how nice.

NICOLE

I wish some other people I know had the same feelings.

MALCOLM

You know what I wish?

NICOLE

What?

MALCOLM

I always wanted a sister. If I had had a sister she would have been like you. You know. Lovable.

NICOLE

How flattering.

MALCOLM

And then I'd fall in love with her and marry her.

NICOLE

That's incest.

MALCOLM

She'd only be a half-sister. Or a step-sister. Besides, love is love. And you and me, we're not related.

NICOLE

Sister love is a very sweet thought.

MALCOLM

And I'd call her honey.

NICOLE

Even sweeter.

MALCOLM

Yes. (*Pleased.*) Candy is dandy but – well, you know. Honey is sweeter than sugar.

NICOLE

And less fattening.

MALCOLM

I get along with you. Do you get along with me?

NICOLE

Well, I suppose if you put it that way.

MALCOLM

Yeah, I like it that we get along together. They tell me I'm naive, but I don't think love is naive. Do you think love is naive?

NICOLE

What's wrong with naive?

MALCOLM

Nothing wrong with it, I guess, as long as you're both in love.

Harvey gets back into the conversation.

HARVEY

(*smiling at the two of them*) Ah, I see things are going well.

NICOLE

Oh, you heard the news too?

HARVEY

Malcolm told me about it – well, hinted at it. Congratulations. I'm very happy for you two.

NICOLE

Congratulations? Actually I'm happier for the girls, to be honest. They could have shut us down!

HARVEY

Over love?

NICOLE

(*with happy irony*) Yeah, "love" is the euphemism for how things happen here, all right.

HARVEY

Well, I don't see why it's any of the girls' business, to be honest. You do what's right for you.

NICOLE

I think it's very much the girls' business. They were the ones involved.

HARVEY

(*perplexed now*) They were involved too? What kind of setup do you guys have anyway? I thought you and Malcolm just met.

NICOLE

We did. What are you talking about?

HARVEY

What are *you* talking about?

MALCOLM

What is this whole conversation about?

Together Harvey and Nicole blurt out:

HARVEY

Love!

NICOLE

Sexually transmitted disease!

> *Harvey stares at them, first at Nicole, then at Malcolm. He turns back to the bar, shaking his head.*

HARVEY

I think I got out on the wrong side of the bed this morning.

NICOLE

This is making me hungry. I'm going to go make a ham sandwich. After that I have to finish the Christmas decorations.

MALCOLM

Mind if I go with you?

NICOLE

Yeah sure, come on.

> *They both leave as ZOE and CRAWFORD enter.*

ZOE

You were a bastard and bastards deserve to suffer. It's a law of life.

CRAWFORD

That law is a new one to me.

ZOE

It's Zoe's law of Crooks and Banks.

> *She turns and goes into her office. Crawford follows. As she goes she turns to Desiree.*

ZOE

Hey, did you forget you have an appointment with Mr. High Flyer?

DESIREE

Oops! (*She leaves for the back.*)

CRAWFORD

Give me a break. Don't you have a heart?

ZOE

Do you have one?

CRAWFORD

What is it you're looking for?

ZOE

Honesty. Just honesty.

CRAWFORD

In this world?

ZOE

How many worlds do you know of?

CRAWFORD

To try to be honest in a dishonest world is like raking leaves against the wind. It's hopeless. You get massacred for being honest.

ZOE

There's a lot of massacring going on anyway.

CRAWFORD

What is it you want, money?

ZOE

Is that all you can think of is money?

CRAWFORD

What do I have to do to convince you I love you?

ZOE

I don't need convincing. I know you love me.

CRAWFORD

Well?

ZOE

Well nothing.

CRAWFORD

Let me do something for you. To prove my love.

ZOE

Sure. If you'll do it.

CRAWFORD

I'll do whatever it is, I promise. If it's in my power.

ZOE

Get that dumb mayor of yours off my back. Him and that even dumber Family Above All. They're like flies. You shoo them away and they come right back again.

CRAWFORD

Zoe, you can't just shoo them away. You have to –

ZOE

Love always finds a way. Especially love combined with money in secret bank accounts.

CRAWFORD

I don't know that the law recognizes love.

ZOE

Which is what's wrong with the law.

CRAWFORD

Ah Zoe, have a heart. Be reasonable.

ZOE

Look, that Mrs. Littletwirp was here –

CRAWFORD

Mrs. Littlefield?

ZOE

– and tried to pin poor old Nanette on me, if you can believe that.

CRAWFORD

(*Laughs*) Nanette? You're kidding! Nanette hasn't worked here in years.

ZOE

Exactly. So if you wanna do something for me, then tell your city hall buddy Stanley Brinkerhoff to tell Mrs. Littleclit to lay off or I'll break my madame-client privilege and tell everybody that her dear late little husband used to come here for all the blow jobs he never got at home.

CRAWFORD

You're kidding! Mortimer Littlefield? Used to come here? I'm shocked.

ZOE

Oh don't be silly. He never came anywhere near here. We'll just start rumors and it'll keep her busy quashing them. Or we can always hope she'll just die of mortification. Anyway, by the time she works her way out of that one, this whole close-the-whorehouse stupidity will have blown over.

CRAWFORD

But Zoe, that's dishonest.

ZOE

Exactly. I'm no more honest than they are. From what I can see, anyone trying to be honest in this town would be left holding the bag.

CRAWFORD

What about your ideals? I've always admired you for your ideals.

ZOE

I have ideals up my yin-yang. But I'll be damned if I'll be left holding the bag. Hanging on to my ideals as crooks close me down? Ha!

CRAWFORD

You know, I'm very shocked.

ZOE

If there's one thing I've learned in life it's that you can have all the ideals you want but don't try to live by them while nobody else is. You have to be careful of your dreams. The more dreams you have, the more dreams that get dashed.

CRAWFORD

Oh that pessimism is so sad. You've been badly hurt. I take full blame for that.

ZOE

Right, and that makes everything all better. You should run for political office. You already have the appropriate degree of dishonesty. All we would have to do now is find you the right governmental slot for your talents. (*Beat*) Of course! Our new banking czar! And that's just for starters. The IMF next! (*Shouts*) Today the IMF, tomorrow the world!

CRAWFORD

You make it a joke.

ZOE

Why not? I'm dishonest too.

CRAWFORD

You?

ZOE

Sex therapy. It's illegal the way I do it.

CRAWFORD

I thought sex therapy was a legitimate profession.

ZOE

Legitimate sex therapy is a legitimate profession but some of the things we do here can get so bizarre they's practically biblical and outside the law. And as for declaring taxes? Let's not talk about them, shall we. You know Gerald? – the accountant?

CRAWFORD

That poor sourpuss bastard? He's hen-pecked. I never once saw him smile in all the years I've known him.

ZOE

That's Gerald, all right. Or rather that was the old Gerald. He gets paid now with discreet little boffs with a girl of his choice. Pussy installments, he calls them. He gets a monthly pussy allowance and calls it bush therapy.

CRAWFORD

I don't think the IRS would like that.

ZOE

You kidding? It's done all over the place. (*Laughs*) The local IRS guy eventually got wind of it and after he got done clucking his tongue at me he told me it was not a financial policy he could endorse. But he liked me and didn't want to report me. (*Laughs*) Poor bastard.

CRAWFORD

That's very nice of him. (*A thought occurs.*) Zoe, wait, this is awful. What are you telling me?

ZOE

You can easily guess what his next move was.

CRAWFORD

No! You don't mean? The IRS guy?

ZOE

Is now a regular. A boff a month. You had to peal his eyes off Hyacinth. He couldn't believe she has a Master's.

CRAWFORD

Hyacinth has a Master's degree?

ZOE

In economics.

CRAWFORD

Then what is she doing here?

ZOE

She says she can make more money as a whore. She's a private contractor here. I must say, we're very lucky having her. She's a regular cash machine. She must radiate something hormonal to men. Anyway, the accountant is an extremely happy man now.

CRAWFORD

Don't tell me any more. You're making me an accessory after the fact.

ZOE

So who's more dishonest here, me or the accountant? Me or the IRS?

> *Desiree reappears. She's dressed in a very handsome flight attendant's uniform.*

Ah, Desiree. (*In appreciation*) Nice. Remember, too much makeup turns him off. And don't forget the turbulence. He loves it when he's in for a bumpy ride and gets tossed all over the bed. Where's your flight attendant's hat? He likes women with hats.

> *Desiree smiles a quick silent greeting to Zoe and Crawford as she walks through and out again.*

CRAWFORD

What was that all about?

ZOE

One of our big clients is due in and he likes flight attendants, Business Class. She's all dressed to give him a great big Christmas present and as much business as he can handle.

CRAWFORD

Oh! That reminds me. I almost forgot. I have a Christmas present for you.

He hands Zoe a large gift-wrapped box.

ZOE

Better not be fur.

CRAWFORD

What's wrong with fur?

ZOE

I don't like animals being killed so women can feel warm.

CRAWFORD

Wouldn't it be nice to have fur during a real Nevada cold spell? What's wrong with that?

ZOE

What's wrong with having an animal's fur during a Nevada cold spell is that it's the animal's fur.

CRAWFORD

Just pulling your leg. This isn't fur – just looks it. Here, let me help you with it on.

ZOE

Oh-h-h. Warm. (*Appreciatively sashays around with it on.*) Ummmmm.

CRAWFORD

Glad you like it, Zoe.

DAWN

(*Half-naked, she runs in agitated.*) Oh Zoe, Mr. Tully wants more champagne. That guy's a schwanz on legs.

ZOE

What do you mean? Aren't you in Room 7? There should be at least six bottles in the fridge.

DAWN

There used to be six bottles in the fridge. That was three toasts ago to the great god Pan. I didn't know gods had pans. What do they use them for?

ZOE

Down the cellar. There's more champagne down the cellar.

> *ZOE and DAWN leave to go get the champagne,*
> *Zoe taking off her new coat as they go.*

YITZAKH

(*from the bar, to Crawford*) What do you do – live here?

CRAWFORD

(*casually politic with Zoe's clientele*) No, I, uh, I'm discussing, uh, a business proposition with management.

YITZAKH

A little late in the day, don't you think?

CRAWFORD

What do you mean?

YITZAKH

There's a rumor going around but we're not supposed to believe it.

CRAWFORD

What rumor's that?

YITZAKH

That the place is closing.

CRAWFORD

Zoe's place? Never.

YITZAKH

You seem pretty sure of it.

CRAWFORD

I'm positive of it.

ZOE

(*coming back through the door and yelling to someone behind her as YITZAKH retreats to the bar*). And tell Mr. Tully there's plenty more champagne where that came from. (*Turning and seeing Crawford*) So where were we? What advice do you have for me? – not that I would trust it. How can you expect anyone to like you if you pull that kind of trick?

CRAWFORD

What kind of trick?

ZOE

Cheating people out of their life money. That kind of trick.

CRAWFORD

Look, what I'm trying to tell you is that what I did was an honest mistake. And I got burned too.

ZOE

An honest mistake? You sound like a politician. Congressmen are always making honest mistakes. And we always end up paying for their mistakes. All they do is get richer with their honest mistakes.

CRAWFORD

Of course it's honest. It's landed me in trouble too. I'm losing my shirt.

ZOE

You deserve to lose your shirt. And your imported French underwear too.

CRAWFORD

It was just that after the crash I thought the Vegas housing market was back again and worth investing in. But I happened to be wrong. People weren't buying houses. It was a bunch of hedge fund people back East who were investing in houses and hoping to make a killing.

ZOE

And?

CRAWFORD

They couldn't find enough renters to make it work, so they pulled out.

ZOE

And?

CRAWFORD

And left me holding the bag.

ZOE

(sweetly but with an edge) A smart guy like you? (then in her natural voice) How did they do that? You make it sound easy – making money.

CRAWFORD

Making money? It is. You buy low and sell high. That's the classic formula for making money, big money – especially if you're a hedge-fund or private-equity manager. You drive the market up on speculative bubbles, cash out before the bubbles burst, and then repurchase the same assets at distressed fire-sale prices after the damage has been done. Some big Wall Street firms made bundles gambling on home mortgages before the 2008 crash. They conveniently sold them before the bottom fell out, then bought up foreclosed properties at low prices and turned them into rental units. Which they then rented right back to some of the same people who could no longer afford owning the homes they once owned. See? Not really crooked and quite easy.

ZOE

Sounds like scalping to me.

CRAWFORD

The New York Times reports that with home prices starting to rise and fewer foreclosed homes available to purchase, several of these financial firms are now moving on to other things. Sub-prime mortgages might even make a comeback. Watch your wallets.

ZOE

All this is over my head.

CRAWFORD

No it really isn't. You design subprime mortgages to fail. Then you bet that they'll fail and you clean up. But that's all ancient history now.

ZOE

Ancient theft, you mean.

CRAWFORD

It's all done with robots these days. A robot will execute tens of thousands of stock market transactions in the time it would take a human trader to blink his eyes once. Ah, but is robot trading available to us? That's the kicker.

ZOE

Where would we get a robot?

CRAWFORD

Exactly. We can't. It's out of our league. What we need to do instead is get into derivatives.

ZOE

Derivatives.

CRAWFORD

You want me to 'splain?

ZOE

It would help.

CRAWFORD

Do you know what a derivative is?

ZOE

What is this, Twenty Questions?

CRAWFORD

It's when you take an asset and sell it.

ZOE

We don't sell assets here. We sell ass.

CRAWFORD

OK, let's say you sell your girls' . . . uh . . . asses and say you call them Love Bonds, OK? You sell somebody ten percent of the House of All Nations Love Bonds. And there you have it. You just sold a derivative.

ZOE

A derivative of what?

CRAWFORD

Of nothing. That's the point.

ZOE

I can't tell you how fascinating this is.

PHIL

(*reading from the paper*) Hey that Daffodil stock just went up again – *wow!* – thirty points. And I was gonna buy some three years ago.

CRAWFORD

(*speaking to Zoe and ignoring Phil*) OK, skip the details. Here's my plan. Get a new hedge fund to buy up Vegas property. You know, what's sauce for the goose is sauce for the gander. Call it Vegas Inc.

ZOE

Where's the money in that?

CRAWFORD

You start a hedge fund and then turn around and sell the whole hedge fund to the Chinese for a quick profit. That'll get us out of the woods. It's all just stuff on paper.

ZOE

You must be joking.

CRAWFORD

No. Leave it to me. Trust me

ZOE

I tried that once.

CRAWFORD

Zoe, have faith in me.

ZOE

I have more faith in a snake. What about the whole foreclosure thing? Shutting us down.

CRAWFORD

That's no problem. You just stop the foreclosure.

ZOE

Oh sure, stop the foreclosure. Hang on while I go get my magic wand.

CRAWFORD

Look, you go to the bank – no, get your lawyers to go to the bank and tell them you demand to see the foreclosure papers. I assure you the whole thing is easy. Talk to Roger Thompson. He's the local manager. Ask if he has the paperwork.

ZOE

What paperwork?

CRAWFORD

The foreclosure papers. You have a right to see them.

ZOE

So I'll see the foreclosure papers.

CRAWFORD

But that's just it, you see?

ZOE

See what?

CRAWFORD

He won't be able to produce them. There won't *be* any foreclosure papers. There never *were* any. Most banks didn't have them, with all those toxic mortgages. They bought and sold titles – names on paper. Some of them didn't even know *what* they bought. They just packaged stuff, gave it a name, and resold it for a profit.

ZOE

Your bank too?

CRAWFORD

Well . . . I uh . . .

ZOE

Are you part of this scam?

CRAWFORD

(*hedging*) I'll tell you what. *I'll* go talk to the bank manager. In fact I have to leave right now anyway but I'll be back. I have an appointment that can't be –

ZOE

If the bank can't produce the title paperwork, it can't foreclose?

CRAWFORD

Right. And you stay open.

ZOE

What about your bank?

CRAWFORD

Well, we're all in this together.

ZOE

(*almost admiringly*) Why you little scam artist. You cute little sonuvabitch. I bet your parents were proud of you.

CRAWFORD

Actually I was born out of wedlock. Long story – I'll tell you some time.

ZOE

(*almost affectionately*) Born out of wedlock. Why you little bastard.

CRAWFORD

And I'll make it up to you.

ZOE

Don't bother. Hey. Don't *you* have a big stake in First Farmers of Nevada?

CRAWFORD

Me and a lot of others. Let's just say if I lose my shirt that's my tough luck.

> *(As they're talking, Malcolm appears in the doorway, looking around stealthily. He whispers.)*

MALCOLM

Nicole . . . Nicole . . .

> *(He turns to leave.)*

CRAWFORD

I've gotta go. Who was that?

ZOE

I don't know but I think we just lost a possible asset.

CRAWFORD

I'll be back. This won't take long. We'll continue this.

> *He leaves.*

MALCOLM

(*hearing them talking has come back in*) Oh, I didn't see you there.

ZOE

Can I be of some help?

MALCOLM

I was looking for Nicole.

ZOE

Are you here for business or for pleasure?

MALCOLM

Oh no, for just purely personal reasons.

ZOE

Well, you know, sex has been known to be pretty personal in moments.

MALCOLM

It's to help with the decorating. We were having a ham sandwich, that is, Nicole was having a ham sandwich and then we were going to finish the Christmas decorations.

ZOE

Where'd she go, then?

MALCOLM

She said she had to go to the ladies room.

ZOE

Do you have to go now too?

MALCOLM

The ladies room? No, I'm OK. I'm told I have a big bladder. She said I'd find the decorations in the back room. All right if I poke around?

ZOE

Sure, go ahead.

MALCOLM

Where's the back room?

ZOE

(*pointing*) Usually in the back.

MALCOLM

Thanks.

ZOE

Just don't go knocking on any doors.

DAWN

(*As Malcolm leaves, Dawn reappears, disheveled but happy.*) Woo-hoo!

ZOE

What now?

DAWN

Mr. Tully wants to try out the Sybian vibrator. He says he's never tried it.

ZOE

Where was it last used? I think in Room Four. But Phil will know. Did you explain to Mr. Tully those things are meant for women? – (*her voice then trails off, pursuing a private thought*). . . although, men, hmmm . . .

DAWN

I told him that. He wants me to try it out while he watches. He says there's nothing more beautiful than a woman in the throes of passion.

ZOE

Around here? You're kidding. There's no passion around here. This is a whorehouse.

DAWN

I love the way he gets all poetic. He says he likes to observe women enjoying their beautiful agony. I didn't know he liked S&M.

> *Dawn leaves. ZOE goes to bar and sits down and NICOLE appears.*

NICOLE

Where's Malcolm?

ZOE

He's looking for you in the Back Room.

NICOLE

I need a break.

> *She gets behind the bar.*

ZOE

Men. What do they understand? They live in a world so limited I wouldn't want any part of it. Everything is work and career. That's all they think about. Money, investments, profits, not feelings. They don't know what love is.

NICOLE

I don't think I would go so far as to say that.

ZOE

(*continuing private thoughts*) A woman would do anything for the man she loves. Where there's love, problems and hardships are nothing.

NICOLE

Well, that I would agree with. Without love life would be bleak.

ZOE

Without love, there *is* no life.

NICOLE

Yes, true, I suppose you could say that. Where there's no love . . .

ZOE

I notice that that fellow – Malcolm? – he's interested in you. Is that true? Such a kid.

NICOLE

(*laughs*) I don't know if he's in love with me.

ZOE

Men are honest when they're that young. No game playing.

NICOLE

You say that because Mr. Crawford has hurt you, but he loves you, you know. And he's not a bad catch.

ZOE

That's such an old fashioned way of thinking about men. Good catch, bad catch. I think of it the other way round. We're a pretty good catch for *them*. What would they do without us?

NICOLE

Well, the two go together.

ZOE

Women sacrifice themselves for a man they love and what do men do? Do you know what Crawford does in his spare time? You'll never guess. He has a hobby.

NICOLE

What's his hobby?

ZOE

Collecting hula hoops.

NICOLE

He collects hula hoops? (*laughs*)

ZOE

He collects hula hoops, especially Australian hula hoops. He has the biggest collection of hula hoops this side of the Mississippi. Maybe both sides of the Mississippi.

The door bursts open and the Mayor comes in, followed by a gangly policeman and a seething Mrs. Littlefield. She is keeping herself under control.

MRS. LITTLEFIELD

There she is!

ZOE

(crossing over, confronting them) What do you mean, charging in like this?

MAYOR

(attempting to sound resolute) We're here to close you down!

ZOE

Oh Stanley! don't be so utterly ridiculous. You know you have no legal right to close me down.

PHIL

Ho ho! What have we here? A touching Christmas gesture. A visit from the forces of law and order? And on the very eve, how nice. Drinks, anyone?

He's ignored.

POLICEMAN

(to Zoe) Madame . . .

ZOE

Oh please. Call me anything you want but don't call me madame.

POLICEMAN

With all due proper notice, I'm here to serve you –

ZOE

Serve shmerve. You have no right to enter here without a warrant –

POLICEMAN

With all due proper notice –

ZOE

– unless, of course you're looking for a good time.

MAYOR

Zoe, I just want to explain –

MRS. LITTLEFIELD

Oh stop it! Stop this farce, <u>all</u> of you. (*to Policeman*) Do your thing. Close this – this – this place of fornication. (*adamantly*) I'm not leaving till the place is shut down.

ZOE

Oh good, you're welcome to stay as long as you like. And if you have no socially transmittable diseases, we could use you as, you know, a mature lady, MILF, in Room Number Five. That's the one with all the mirrors. I'll phone Dr. Smedley to arrange for your tests.

MRS. LITTLEFIELD

Ugh!

ZOE

No, wait! Room Four! The new Dildo Room for those of advanced tastes. Have you ever tried a Sybian?

MRS. LITTLEFIELD

This is really too . . . !

MAYOR

(*prodding the policeman*) Go on, do your thing.

POLICEMAN

Madame . . .

ZOE

Again madame! *Must* you? And anyhow, what grounds do you have for even being here – unless you're here as clients? In which case you'll need to pass a dick check. Oh, and uh (*looking at Mayor Brinkerhoff*), on the plus side, this week we're offering a discount on Viagra.

MAYOR

(*To the policeman.*) Tell them. Go on, tell them what we were discussing.

POLICEMAN

Your Honor, to go into subjects as discussed would take us into matters of speculation, which it's not my place to do that. But I can conclude that upon arrival at the scene and observing the premises and its occupants . . .

ZOE

Oh cut the horse shit!

MAYOR

Horse shit?!

Coral dashes in.

ZOE

(to Coral) Oh no! Don't tell me he wants more champagne. What are you all doing in there, taking champagne baths?

CORAL

The Sybian's not working.

ZOE

Oh! That Dawn!

CORAL

I don't think it was one of Dawn's marathons. She has interesting hobbies but that's not one of them. I think it was the movie people here last week. A whole gang of them.

MAYOR

What movie people?

CORAL

Hollywood. They're making a movie called "Holy Madonna".

POLICEMAN

(in quiet amazement in spite of himself) They're making a movie about Madonna? Already?

MAYOR

Hollywood people? here?

CORAL

A certain well-known film studio that shall remain nameless has a house account here.

ZOE

(*admonishing Coral*) Why don't you give out phone numbers while you're at it?

CORAL

Oh Zoe, the whole world knows movie stars are some of our best clients. (*amiably*) And they tip well too.

MAYOR

(*meditatively*) Wow. Hollywood stars – right here. Right where we're standing.

ZOE

Calm down, Stanley. Hollywood people don't vote in Nevada. They vote in California.

PHIL

Hey, get this. (*Reads headline from newspaper.*) Mayor Unveils Erection to Cheering Crowd.

ZOE

Oh that's a good one!

MAYOR

Oh see here now!

Crawford returns.

ZOE

Back so soon?

CRAWFORD

I forgot to take my –. Hey, what's going on here?

POLICEMAN

Mr. Crawford! I didn't know that you, uh – you, I mean – here – I mean, I didn't know that you too – in a place like this –

CRAWFORD

(*quashing him*) Oh nonsense, you still don't know I'm here. What the hell is this policeman doing here?

MRS. LITTLEFIELD

(*jumping in*) It's to close down this den of sin. Tell him, officer. Go on! Tell him!

CRAWFORD

In the first place, it's not a den and in the second place, nobody's closing anything down. How many times do we have to go through all this nonsense? You may not think so, but Zoe, that is, Mrs. Muhlbach here, is a respectable woman.

MRS. LITTLEFIELD

Ugh!

CRAWFORD

A woman of great virtue.

MRS. LITTLEFIELD

Which is why she operates this den of iniquity.

CORAL

(*smarting from Mrs. Littlefield's slight*) What do you mean iniquity? We're perfectly respectable whores.

MRS. LITTLEFIELD

(*venomously*) A h*ouse of prostitution!*

CORAL

(*as though by rote*) We're private contractors practicing a recognized profession that provides a community service.

MRS. LITTLEFIELD

And sexually transmits disease.

CORAL

We, at least, are tested once a week. When was the last time you had *your* twat looked at?

MRS. LITTLEFIELD

Oh how disgusting!

CORAL

It is? Well don't look at it so close up next time.

ZOE

Everyone! Let's all just calm down. (*to CORAL*) Explain to Mr. Tully that we'll get to the Sybian problem as soon as we can and meanwhile he'll have to make do with the usual human methods.

Loud womanly screams from within.

ZOE

Sounds like they're doing quite well with usual human methods.

More shouts.

CORAL

(*excitedly leaving,* saying as she goes) Hey, I want some of this.

PHIL

(*warmly appreciatively*) There's no greater joy than fulfillment.

More shouts.

PHIL

Happiness!

MRS. LITTLEFIELD

Filth!

PHIL

Orgasms!

MRS. LITTLEFIELD

Orgasms detached from love are an empty experience.

PHIL

Well, you know, one man's meat . . .

MRS. LITTLEFIELD

Oh don't be trite! This is all so sordid. I should never have come to this horrid place. Come, Stanley, let us go.

ZOE

(*to the mayor*) Stanley – I mean, Mr. Brinkerhoff –

MAYOR

Yes?

ZOE

I think you may have been misled. To close us down you need legal authorization from the state's attorney general. Do you have one?

MAYOR

Of course we have a state's attorney general.

ZOE

No, authorization papers.

MAYOR

Of course I do.

CRAWFORD

May we see them?

MAYOR

See what?

CRAWFORD

The authorization.

MAYOR

Uh – I have it in my office.

MALCOLM

(*coming back in*) Oh uh am I interrupting anything?

CRAWFORD

Yes.

MAYOR

(*In a pleading tone*) No! Come in! Come in!

NICOLE

You looking for me?

MALCOLM

Ah, there you are. Uh, I was hoping to see you alone.

NICOLE

Sounds exciting!

ZOE

Everybody clear out. I've had enough of these shenanigans.

MRS. LITTLEFIELD

As indeed have I.

CRAWFORD

Mrs. Littlefield, I wish you would reconsider your position. What Zoe does may be repugnant to someone of your, shall we say, refined sensibilities, but perhaps you might think of it as a service to our little community.

MRS. LITTLEFIELD

Hmpf! You mean disgrace.

CRAWFORD

And besides, if I recall correctly, Family Above All has the backing of First Farmers.

MRS. LITTLEFIELD

That's just a little loan technicality.

CRAWFORD

A big technicality – say a hundred grand loan.

MRS. LITTLEFIELD

We – that is –

CRAWFORD

Mrs. Littlefield, your financial affairs will be safe. I think I'm still in a position to give you my personal assurance. (*Turning to Mayor*) Stanley, go get the authorization. If it exists.

MAYOR

Of course it exists. I uh . . . (*To Mrs. Littlefield as they go out*) Perhaps we should leave these . . . uh . . . premises?

MRS. LITTLEFIELD

Not a moment too soon.

CRAWFORD

(*calling after them*) Zoe and I will wait right here till you get back.

> *He and ZOE go into her office. Zoe pours them*
> *drinks as the action continues at the bar.*

MALCOLM

They all seem upset about something.

NICOLE

Don't give it another thought.

MALCOLM

It's nice being alone with you.

NICOLE

(*teasingly*) Oo!

MALCOLM

I just want to tell you how deeply I feel for you but I don't have the words.

NICOLE

You don't need any more words than that.

MALCOLM

Yes but I'd like to say I love you.

NICOLE

(*laughs*) You just did.

MALCOLM

Oh. (*Thinks for a moment.*) Oh.

NICOLE

And I'm touched.

MALCOLM

Have *you* ever been in love before?

NICOLE

I don't believe I have – not really. What do you say, do you think we should get on with the decorations?

MALCOLM

I love Christmas, don't you?

They leave.

YITZAKH

(*to Dikran*) Ah! Love! (*getting no response*) Hey, you awake!

DIKRAN

Why? What difference would it make?

YITZAKH

Why are you do depressed?

DIKRAN

I'm not depressed. I'm a realist. Don't you see what's happening to mankind?

As Dikran says this, Coral wanders in. She's practically naked. Seats herself at the bar.

CORAL

What's happening to mankind?

YITZAKH

What are you doing here? Did you get kicked out? I thought you were having a good time in there.

CORAL

Boy was I ever. But Mr. Tully is, shall we say, very busy and I was getting a little lonesome. Voyeurism is not my thing. I'm more of an action person.

YITZAKH

Hey, Coral. Do mankind a favor and give my friend here a little action.

CORAL

That's what we're here for. (*to Dikran*) Hi, sailor.

DIKRAN

Why do you call me sailor? Even just thinking of the sea makes me seasick.

CORAL

Just a friendly greeting. You look like you could use a friend.

DIKRAN

I'm not dumb. You want to get me in the sack.

CORAL

How perverse of me. I must be some kind of heterosexual or something. Anyway, I just wanted to ask you about Armenia. You know, like, where is it?

DIKRAN

It's in any atlas. Books. Remember books?

CORAL

You ever want to go there and see it?

DIKRAN

I've thought about it.

CORAL

Why don't you want to go to bed with me?

DIKRAN

I've thought about that too.
CORAL
You have? Well well well. And what was the verdict?

DIKRAN

I'm still in deep mourning.

CORAL

I respect that. But maybe a few moments of happiness might be just the thing.

DIKRAN

In a way you remind me of my wife.

CORAL

(*a ray of hope*) Really? In what way?

DIKRAN

You don't have false teeth, do you?

CORAL

(*horrified*) No! Good grief! Why do you ask *that*?

DIKRAN

No, it's only because she didn't have false teeth either. So I just wanted to be sure. I mean because you look like you have the same kind of figure in a way. And I'm glad you still have all your teeth. She did too. Every time I look at you I think of her.

CORAL

I'm flattered. There's a very easy way to find out if there's a resemblance. Including a full set of teeth.

DIKRAN

How?

CORAL

Follow me. I'll show you.

DIKRAN

Show me how?

CORAL

We'll have a private viewing. We'll compare my figure with hers. (*Taunting him.*) You're not afraid to be alone with me, are you?

DIKRAN

(*challenged*) Who me? No. I – uh . . .

CORAL

Come on, then.

> *Hugging his arm, she overcomes the last of his weakening resistance and they leave.*

HYACINTH

(*staggers in*) I must admit, that Mr. Tully is a handful.

YITZAKH

Still going at it?

HYACINTH

I thought only females got in heat. Phew!

MAYOR

(*rushes back breathlessly*)

HYACINTH

Well, look who's here. And today's not his day.

ZOE

(*coming out of her office*) The man with the important documents.

MAYOR

That is to say ...

ZOE

(*happily*) What, no papers? Don't tell me.

HYACINTH

Of course there aren't any papers.

CRAWFORD

(*accompanying ZOE*) No, of course not. They've been passed on from bank to financial institution to other banks and probably can never be found or traced, even assuming they existed.

MAYOR

But the place *is* foreclosed. Maybe the papers aren't immediately available but on my honor as mayor –

HYACINTH

Can it, your honor.

MAYOR

Can it? I – that is –

HYACINTH

It's no longer foreclosed. I paid the mortgage.

MAYOR

Hunh? You what?

ZOE

You *what*?!

CRAWFORD

I don't get it.

ZOE

Yeah. What's going on?

HYACINTH

A few years back one of my favorite clients gave me some shares in a start-up computer company as a tip. I guess I must have put him in a real happy mood and as a small token of appreciation he gave me twenty shares of stock in a small unknown company.

ZOE

Twenty shares of stock! You call that a small token?

HYACINTH

For services rendered. He said he'd propose to me but he was already married and had been married eight times before that and his faith in marriage vows was getting a little shaky.

ZOE

Well I never! What services did you render? Something on our special menu? Or was this al fresco?

HYACINTH

This one's definitely not on our menu but (*looking around*) I can't discuss it publicly for professional reasons.

ZOE

(*in support of Hyacinth*) Of course, we're all professionals here. Discretion is our motto.

CRAWFORD

That's a lot of stock. (*admiringly*) This girl's got hidden talents.

ZOE

(*with pride*) We have high standards here.

CRAWFORD

Still, that's a tremendous amount of stock, though. This gentleman was crazy enough to give you twenty shares of a company?

HYACINTH

Back then they were only worth something like fifty dollars a share, so it was a nice generous thousand-dollar tip. But within a year the stock went up up up, split twice and has since split two more times and before you knew it I was rolling in it.

CRAWFORD

You make Wall Street sound like a gambling casino.

HYACINTH

Well it's not exactly your local bridge club.

CRAWFORD

(*disbelief*) And you made money after all that subprime meltdown horror?

HYACINTH

I did a lot of reading, you know, little financial blogs on the internet – learned the ropes. I bought bank stocks when they were low and banks were getting bailed out by the Federal Reserve. Then sold them when they started climbing and at the same time shorted some hot traditional stocks, invested in the Euro and with the various proceeds bought some more Daffodil. Simple. Once you have money it's easy to make money.

CRAWFORD

What? You own shares of Daffodil Computers?

HYACINTH

Five thousand shares.

CRAWFORD

Five thou –! You know what Daffodil is going for these days?

HYACINTH

It closed yesterday at, I think, one forty-five.

PHIL

(*calling over, holding the newspaper up*) A hundred and fifty. One five oh.

ZOE

Holy smoholy!

PHIL

It's that new version of an iPhone they're coming out with. A kind of a pocket TV plus film library.

ZOE

You know what that means?

CRAWFORD

It means we're indebted to her.

HYACINTH

(*smiling sweetly*) Actually in a sense I own you all. Well, the premises anyway.

ZOE

O my God! Hyacinth!

CRAWFORD

A hundred and fifty times five thousand shares is uh –

HYACINTH

(*taking out a hand calculator*) Seven hundred and fifty thousand dollars.

ZOE

(*lovingly*) My dear, that must make you just about the richest piece of ass in Las Vegas.

HYACINTH

(*happily agreeing*) Uh-hunh.

CRAWFORD

In all of Nevada!

MAYOR

In the whole Southwest! Er, from what I hear.

ZOE

(*worried*) What are you going to do?

HYACINTH

After the burn-the-mortgage party?

ZOE

Yes.

HYACINTH

Have a bang-up Christmas party, drinks on the house.

MAYOR

(*happily entering into the spirit of the fun*) And a free lay for everybody! (*aware of what he just said but not really caring*) Well, you know . . .

ZOE

(teasing *the mayor*) What do you think this is, the Red Cross?

MAYOR

Er –

ZOE

(*to Hyacinth*) So now you're running the whole show.

HYACINTH

Naa. After the mortgage business I'll still have enough left over to do what I want. And being a madam is not high on my list.

CRAWFORD

So what do you want?

HYACINTH

Go back to school and get my PhD.

CRAWFORD

In what?

HYACINTH

Economics.

ZOE

(*beams at her*) We have nothing but the best here.

CRAWFORD

Just when you think you have everybody figured out.

ZOE

What's to figure out? Men are what they are and women are what they are.

CRAWFORD

I don't know what else we can be.

ZOE

You kidding? We could all be better.

CRAWFORD

(*to Zoe*) Looks like you're still in business.

ZOE

Yep. Zoe's good old-fashioned cathouse.

HYACINTH

The House of All Nations.

CRAWFORD

So here we go again. In a sense it's the eternal return. Fundamentals never change.

HYACINTH

History repeats itself and if it's good it'll come back.

ZOE

If it's bad it comes back faster.

PHIL

It all comes back. You just wait and see. People are new in each generation and create the same mess all over again. I was just reading a headline this morning: "Psychics Predict World Didn't End Yesterday." (*laughs*) That was a good one.

CRAWFORD

Where do you get this stuff from?

PHIL

Newspaper headlines. I have a lot of fun with headlines.

MALCOLM

(*coming back with an arm lovingly around Nicole*) Wow. Looks like a party going on.

NICOLE

Yes! And don't the decorations look just beautiful!

ZOE

Hey, all we're missing now is Mr. Tully.

HYACINTH

Mr. Tully's going to be busy for quite a while. He's trying something different. It's some Viennese trick he said he found in Krafft-Ebing.

HARVEY

(*coming to life*) Hey, that could be interesting.

ZOE

(*laughs, happily impressed*) Bless you, you're ready to go again.

HARVEY

(*seized by modesty*) Wa-al you know . . .

DIKRAN and CORAL appear, Dikran with a happy grin.

DIKRAN

(*looking surprised to see the group, he turns to Coral*) It certainly was great but I didn't expect a welcoming committee.

CORAL

Oh don't mind the crowd.

ZOE

Yeah, don't mind us, we're celebrating. Come on, I'll buy you a drink.

DIKRAN

What an establishment! First you get laid, then they give you a free drink.

ZOE

Only on Christmas.

YITZAKH

(*coming over from the bar*) And what about Chanukah? What is this, more discrimination?

ZOE

(*Turns toward Crawford and playfully punches his stomach.*) Come on, you little bastard.

DIKRAN

Wow, this is some cathouse! I had no idea.

ZOE

(*as the curtain starts to fall*) You kidding? Listen, the whole world's a cathouse.

CURTAIN

www.ingramcontent.com/pod-product-compliance
Lightning Source LLC
Chambersburg PA
CBHW080522030426
42337CB00023B/4601